NOW
IS THE TIME!

Building Community Resilience in Response
to COVID-19 and the Climate Crisis

To Charmaine

Best Fred

FRED IRWIN

Tellwell Talent
www.tellwell.ca

ISBN
978-0-2288-5320-6 (Paperback)
978-0-2288-5321-3 (eBook)

DEDICATION

With my love and gratitude, I dedicate this book to my three sons and six grandchildren, that they may find ways to navigate through COVID-19 and the climate crisis, celebrating life and contributing to the greater good beyond their own self-interest.

SPECIAL THANKS

To my partner, Judy Shonbeck, who assisted me daily during the pandemic to help organize our time, keep us both healthy, and share simple pleasures, I extend my love and gratitude.

TABLE OF CONTENTS

Introduction xi

Chapter 1 Now is the Time! 1

Original Article, April 2020 1

Follow-On Commentary, December 2020 7

Chapter 2 Post Carbon Chatter 10

Foreward, December 2020 10

Our Casino Economy 14

It's Oil, Stupid! 17

The Fox and the Hare 19

What Energy Crisis! 21

The Bursting Carbon Bubble 23

Bold & Local Economic Infrastructure 25

Global Fire, Local GEM 27

Living Locally 29

Local Food Security 34

2% Municipal Solution 36

My Life Story on Energy 38

Follow-On Commentary, End Of December 2020 42

**Chapter 3 Renewable Power Generation
Investment Trust Fund**.. 47

Concept Proposal to the City of Peterborough.......................... 47

Follow-up email letter to the PDI Investment Options
Working Group with respect to the virtual meeting
and presentation on Friday, August 7, 2020 59

Trent Community Research Centre (TCRC) Project # 4874 ... 62

Chapter 4 Strategic Roadmap 64

Executive Summary 64

A. Introduction 69

B. Now Is the time!.. 71

C. Renewable Energy Investment...................................... 72

D. Resiliency Imperative Changing Lifestyles................... 77

E. Permaculture Operating System 79

F. 4 E's Framework 82

G. Leadership.. 84

H. Localization Strategy.. 85

I. Economic Localization Infrastructure........................... 96

J. Environment.. 98

K. Social & Economic Equity 100

L. 10 Key Actions on the Resiliency Timeline 101

M. Attached Appendix... 103

Chapter 5 Think Resilience 105

Think Resilience Strategy Proposal 105

Think Resilience Proposal Video Presentation Outline 110

Commentary on the Strategy Proposal 123

Chapter 6 Advancing into the Age of Resilience 125

The Sustainable Development Myth 125

The Energy Crisis Arrives with Peak Conventional
Oil in 2006 129

Fracking for Oil & Gas Reboots Economic Growth 130

Building Resilience at Community Level 133

Global Environmental Sustainability Movement Has Failed.... 134

The Paris Climate Accord 136

Will the US Re-Joining the Paris Climate Accord
Make a Difference?.. 138

Will Switching to Renewables Solve the Emissions
Predicament?...141

Is Nuclear Power a Viable Option?............................141

What about the Hydrogen Economy and Fuel Cells? 145

More on the Environmental Sustainability Movement............147

Bouncing Forward with Permaculture into the Age of
Resilience 149

Chapter 7 Permaculture Regenerative Systems 154

Foreward.. 154

Energy Descent Regenerative System 160

Local Renewable Power Regenerative System 167

Economic Localization Infrastructure Regenerative System 169

Kawartha Loon local currency 169

Investing, Buying, and Trading Locally....................172

Local Investing...174

Local Food, Water and Wellness 176

Downtown Culture Hub 183

Environmental Regenerative Systems 185

Equity Regenerative Systems 186

Peterborough Community Goals 190

Chapter 8 My Last Words...191

Notes and References 193

Introduction 193

Chapter 1 194

Chapter 2 194

Chapter 3 198

Chapter 4 199

Chapter 5 201

Chapter 6 201

Chapter 7 202

[Handwritten note: Missing is the equity piece → mention economic equity ⊕ about Indigenous Voices or those of POC]

INTRODUCTION

December 2020

The COVID-19 news seems so threatening and numbing. We, in Peterborough, Ontario, about one hundred kilometers northeast of Toronto, are so fortunate in our relative isolation. Having worked and lived in the USA for eighteen years in two different employment stints with Fortune 500 companies, both with global responsibilities, I remain hooked on US news. Isolated still further in our small cottage twenty kilometers or so from Peterborough City Hall, my partner Judy and I were shocked months ago when the US death toll passed thirty thousand. We have been in self-isolation ever since, connected by the internet with Zoom, Facebook, and email, supplemented by the local daily newspaper and more TV than ever before.

Transition Town Peterborough (TTP) was started by a small group of dedicated volunteers in 2007 when I was my partner Judy's age today and we are both now in the COVID-19 vulnerable age group and are both anxiously awaiting our turn for the vaccine. We guesstimate that will be around mid-March. We are safe and secure and grateful to be healthy and alive. I will share much more about TTP as we proceed but suffice to say that we were moving along quite well through 2019, continuing with our two annual festivals and communicating with our supporters through our quarterly print publication, *Greenzine*, a magazine dedicated to "Building Our Local Living Economy," then COVID-19 hit and changed everything.

As I looked out our pitch-black front window before dinner, Judy reminded me that today was the winter solstice. Wolf Blitzer, CNN Situation Room at 6:00 pm, reported total US deaths had reached nearly 320,000. Further, the UK was in lock down because of a new, more contagious strain of the virus while the second vaccine from Moderna rolled out across America at "Warp Speed," which was the name of the US government's program to advance the production of COVID-19 vaccines. The first shipment of Pfizer vaccines had just arrived in Canada.

Meanwhile, Canada cut off air travel with the UK, and US President-Elect Biden received his first vaccine shot while President Trump held up in the White House reportedly discussing the possibility of enforcing martial law in those swing states that voted for Biden in an attempt to overthrow the election of the Biden-Harris ticket----Oh yeah, the US Congress is about to approve an emergency relief bill of US $900 billion to help feed and support the millions of Americans who are now food insecure.

Our local morning newspaper announced Canadian PM Justin Trudeau's new plan to increase the carbon tax in increments hitting five-year emissions targets starting in 2035, and net-zero carbon by 2050. Politics will likely take the carbon tax to the Canadian Supreme Court, and the plan itself supporting wind and solar renewable energy and even small nuclear energy may trigger a vote of no-confidence early in the new year leading to a 2021 Canadian federal election.

That is a little political speculation on my part, however, the newly elected leader of the Federal Conservative Party of Canada, Her Majesty's Official Opposition to the Federal Liberal Government of Canada is already positioning to campaign in the next election on the need for the Canadian government to rein in the budget deficit and practice more austerity before PM Justin Trudeau "bankrupts the country."

It seems that conservatives on both sides of the US/Canada border are more concerned with bankrupting their respective countries than they are in the health and welfare of their own people during these unprecedented times of a global pandemic and the climate crisis.

Neither conservative party recognizes that as sovereign nations with their own fiat currency neither the USA nor Canada can go bankrupt. It's not for a shortage of money that so many have been allowed to die from COVID-19 or so many of the living in both countries are food insecure and some are starving.

As the founder of the Kawartha Loon (KL) local currency issued by TTP, I am the receiver of a steady diet of people who know more about money than I do and can set the record straight. We will come back to the KL local currency in this book. If you are interested in how money is created and how it works, the best most recent book recommendation that I can make is for *The Deficit Myth: Modern Monetary Theory and the Birth of the People's Economy* by Stephanie Kelton. Of course, you have to read it and understand how money is created and how the Canadian and US governments actually come up with all the money for COVID-19 relief--- It's not from your taxes as you may think!

This is all to say that these are not ordinary times. But then we are not at all certain what ordinary times will ever look like again. Nonetheless, if you would have asked me what kind of book I might want to write during my last year as an active part of Team Transition and the TTP's board of directors it would certainly include recognition for our many volunteers and people who have served year after year on our operating committees for the Transition Skills Forum, the Purple Onion Harvest Festival, the Dandelion Day Festival, the Kawartha Loon Exchange Board of Governors, the *Greenzine* Editorial Collective, Local Food Month, Resilient Ptbo 2030, Transition Neighbourhoods Project, 50% Local Food 2030 and all of the thousands of transitioners who have attended so many of our festivals, town halls, meetups and forums as well as the five thousand people each quarter who received our *Greenzine* magazine.

For certain, we need to celebrate their support and their engagement in our mission to help build a community of greater resilience and happiness. However, that book remains to be written.

As I said, COVID-19 changed everything. Our board of directors was early to cancel the new spring festival, called the Peter Patch LocalPalooza, scheduled for late-June 2020. Shortly after that, we cancelled the second quarter of the *Greenzine* magazine and then the 10th Annual Purple Onion Harvest Festival scheduled for the end of September 2020, and finally, we were forced to shut down the *Greenzine* print magazine as our major source of income and connection to five thousand households each quarter. Back issues of *Greenzine* are available on the TTP website.

Transition Town Peterborough's focus throughout 2020 moved rather swiftly to COVID-19 and the climate crisis as presented in this book. The book is sometimes repetitive with the presentation of real articles and documents as our thinking has progressed and also as a form of communication on the seriousness and difficulty with which the idea of building community resilience really is.

We evolve in real-time in this book, starting to "bounce forward" into a prioritized number of interactive permaculture regenerative systems requiring the support of everyone in the community over an extended period of time in this long emergency. The regenerative systems of which we speak address our energy, economy, environment and equity, both social and economic.

We hope that you enjoy our journey. Transition Town Peterborough thanks everyone who is motivated by anything in this book that encourages them to join together and share with their fellow citizens to advance their own community's resilience--- Together, we can!

CHAPTER 1
NOW IS THE TIME!

ORIGINAL ARTICLE, APRIL 2020

Now is the time to come together while socially apart. It's time to realize that we are our own destiny and the only intelligence behind the fate of Gaia.

Now is the time for each and every community on earth to integrate its own COVID-19 recovery plan with its own climate crisis plan, as the cause of both is rooted in the collective behaviour of the whole of humanity that continues to harvest more than its fair share of the earth's nutrients for Gaia to sustain its balance and save us from ourselves.

No one is to blame, but everyone must share the blame and come together as one family, one neighbourhood, one community. Now is the time!

Now is the time to realize, as it has always been, that it is the strength of families and neighbourhoods then communities that allow cities to form and then states to organize collective defences. However, the enemies are no longer those with a nuclear arsenal or even those with the ability to conduct cyber warfare; and arguably not even a novel virus or the climate crisis, but rather, it's all about our own human behaviour.

That is, what we can do as neighbourhoods and communities if our life depended on it is precisely what we must do to recover from COVID-19 and the climate crisis. Why? Well, because our lives do actually depend on it!

The "Resiliency Imperative" of our time, for all of us on this planet, is to focus on building our resilience of life essentials---the productive efficiency and security of all forms of energy, fresh water, our food supply, our personal, family, neighbourhood, and our community wellness, as well as the essential best of our social and economic culture--- and, we have to do it all with much greater social and economic equity or much of our individual and collective efforts will be lost.

No part of this is an original thought and all of it has been written more eloquently in countless books. By now there are also hundreds of frameworks on how to change the state to combat climate change and even on how to build retro suburbia, smart communities, sustainable communities, resilient communities, sponge cities, on and on.

What is different now is the shock of the COVID-19 pandemic.

Many of us engaged in working to limit ecological destruction with rising CO_2 emissions anticipated that some significant event that touched all of humanity was likely in the making. However, some have been surprised and blindsided by the COVID-19 virus as our generational global marker.

I have written about personal and system shocks for nearly 50 years.

I have called them SEEs for significant emotional events. They are markers that change the course of events for individuals, families, communities and countries. In the last century, for many it was the Second World War. I have often referenced my personal SEE in 1972 with my diagnosis of rheumatoid arthritis--- It has governed my working career and every behaviour I have ever had since that time--- I thought I was dying from so much prolonged pain. However, I have learned how to live and cope with my pain, be grateful every day and give back to the best of my energy and ability--- but not without more than one magical drug. I cherish hope!

So, I am suggesting that the COVID-19 pandemic is much more than a shock. It's a SEE to me and, I suspect, much of humanity who now live in fear of dying from this mysterious thing. It's emotional and heart-wrenching for those who lose loved ones, family and friends. It's a giant global SEE with no true recovery plan in sight and no magical drug for us all until a vaccine becomes widely available across the globe--- and will it work for all of us and for how long? Nobody knows.

We all hang poised with hope and the support of Andrea Bocelli's beautiful heart-wrenching "Ave Maria" from Milan, Italy, in the midst of the pandemic.

But now is also the time to think about the COVID-19 recovery plan as part of the climate crisis recovery plan of the City and County of Peterborough in Ontario, Canada.

Adopting the Resiliency Imperative ... Committing to Build Community Resilience:

"Resilience is the capacity of a system to encounter disruption and still maintain its base structure and function" (Richard Heinberg, Post Carbon Institute).

The smallest functioning human system is the tribe, or in today's world, the neighbourhood. Neighbourhoods come together and form communities. The community is the building block foundation of every province, state, indigenous nation, and country in the world.

Helping to build community resilience against the likes of COVID-19 and the destructive forces caused by the climate crisis is the mission of TTP and of the Transition Towns movement around the world as founded by Rob Hopkins in 2005.

The City of Peterborough recognized TTP twelve years ago as Canada's first Transition Town and now is asking for the City and County of Peterborough to commit to adopting community resilience as its goal and to become the most Resilient Community in Canada by 2030.

Permaculture Operating System

With such a lofty mission as exists within the Transition Towns movement, we needed a foundational operating system with a set of values and ethics. That operating system is permaculture which is not only related to more permanent agriculture systems that preserve the soil and provide much greater food production than industrial farming practices but also refers to system design practices for communities and cities and a set of values and ethical practices for human behaviour aligned with natural systems.

There simply is no hope for the process of building community resilience in the face of COVID-19 or the worst effects of the climate crisis without a fully integrated operating and design system.

We are therefore asking the City and County of Peterborough to adopt permaculture as their operating system and decision-making lens and, further, to provide funding for key management personnel to be trained in the discipline, not just a sustainability manager but key operational managers, councillors, wardens and mayors.

Transition Town Peterborough has trained hundreds of local citizens in basic permaculture design systems since its inception who will happily support this recommendation--- they are by now transitioners.

Adopt the 4 E's as the Strategic System Framework: Energy, Economy, Environment, Equity

Before moving to recovery plans that can change human behaviour for the greater good, we need a strategic system framework to guide us and simplify our thinking and actions.

The framework is very simple. It identifies that every action towards building a resilient community affects every other part of the system in some way. The four parts of the system framework are energy, economy, environment and equity, both social and economic.

The 4 E's Framework has been a part of the Transition Towns model since its inception. Many other organizations around the world have adopted it. It was the foundation for the document titled, "The Strategic Framework for the Economic Localization of the City and County of Peterborough," as released by TTP in November 2013. This document led to the introduction of the KL local currency, Canada's first fully monetized complementary currency as a fundamental piece of economic localization infrastructure. It also outlined the need for an operating trust owned by the

City and County to non-politically and equitably allocate funds to build local resilience, engaging and leveraging not-for-profit organizations, citizens at large and locally owned businesses and farming enterprises.

The same document also introduced the first energy descent program required to build community resilience. That energy descent program, now branded the Transition Neighbourhoods Project (TNP), is fundamental to economic localization and job creation. It applies to the heating, ventilation and air-conditioning (HVAC) energy sector, the local food human energy and economic sectors, as well as the huge need for much greater social and economic equity in the City of Peterborough, which is currently ranking very high on the list of the most food-insecure cities in Canada.

The City of Peterborough provided modest financial support for the pilot development of the TNP but in the final 2020 budget, rejected the design phase funding with no explanation--- then COVID-19 arrived to dominate our very existence and understandably our total global focus switched to fighting the new enemy--- unfortunately leaving the real common enemy, our collective human behaviour in total limbo--- allowing that to continue could prove disastrous for Peterborough and so many small cities around the world--- economic consolidation around big banks and big corporations will predictably greatly diminish the small locally-owned business sector if we choose not to focus our resources and fight for the economic soul of our community.

That is why as we lead into the plans section; we recognize that most of the successful COVID-19 and climate crisis initiatives are in fact economic behavioural modification---almost every one of them.

Recovery Plans in support of ResilientPtbo 2030

In January 2019, Transition Town Peterborough introduced ResilientPtbo 2030 (RP 2030) with three in-house initiatives utilizing the permaculture model for building resilient communities, including an energy descent initiative, a major new program focusing on local food and, finally, a leading new piece of economic localization infrastructure to increase the circulation of funds in our local community ... a key to local job creation building community resilience along the way.

These programs are:

Transition Neighbourhoods Project (TNP) as an energy descent initiative at the household level utilizing behavioural economics.

Electronic Kawartha Loon (eKL) as a loyalty program to help locally owned businesses and especially local farmers and local food businesses selling into our local community to compete with larger corporations that continue to suck our money and soul from our community.

50% Local Food 2030 has to be our goal if we are to become more food secure with social equity. COVID-19 has exposed the total inadequacy of our local food-supply chain. Without immediate and substantial municipal intervention, the next climate-induced disaster could prove unbearable.

Transition Town Peterborough reached out on RP 2030 with five feedback sessions at the Peterborough Public Library and with a ResilientPtbo 2030 pavilion at the 9th Annual Purple Onion Harvest Festival (POHF) held in September 2019. Local citizens strongly support more municipal funding for local food supporting initiatives.

The 2019 "ResilientPtbo 2030" *Greenzine* edition published in the first quarter of 2019 featured these three initiatives in greater detail and suggested that this was the start of the new plans process to build a much more resilient community.

The 2020 "ResilientPtbo 2030" *Greenzine* edition published in the first quarter of 2020 expanded to introduce many ideas and possible initiatives outside of TTP's capacity to explore more deeply--- calling out for more community support.

Now is the time to take action--- Together, we can!

FOLLOW-ON COMMENTARY, DECEMBER 2020

The "Now is the Time" article was submitted to the City of Peterborough mayor, the 10 City councillors, and to the County warden and two First Nations chiefs in April 2020. It was also distributed via email to a significant number of transitioners in the Community.

Before the submission, City Council had officially declared a climate emergency, but overnight COVID-19 replaced the climate emergency as the focus for both the City and County. Both joined together and formed the COVID-19 Economic Recovery Task Force chaired jointly by the City mayor and County warden and headed by the president of Peterborough & the Kawarthas Economic Development (PKED), which is funded jointly by the City and County of Peterborough.

The COVID-19 pandemic allowed the City mayor to invoke official emergency powers to order changes in bus routes as one example and generally to implement short-term safety measures to continue business transactions as much as possible and to generally react and try to put out the fires wherever. This was no surprise as it was much like the situation in every large and small city in the world.

These emergency powers created a lot of confusion with the public. By this time, City and County Council meetings were virtual but councillors and the mayor were soon overwhelmed with a wide variety of citizen complaints and inquiries. Despite all of this Peterborough fared relatively well with the leadership of the local health unit and the mayor and warden making decisions on the fly and the community coming together with multiple safety nets for less fortunate citizens.

However, as the saying goes--- something had to give--- and that was our collective attention to the City's self-proclaimed climate emergency. The year 2020 will likely turn out to be one of the hottest years on record, and we will have lost at least a full year in our mission to create a more resilient community. The Peterborough Environmental Advisory Committee of Council shut down during the pandemic and remains so at this writing, and with the sole environmental manager in the City also mysteriously leaving her position, there continues to be no focus for climate emergency action ideas and requests.

The City budget for 2021 consumed hours and hours of work by Council and staff during the pandemic. Creating this budget was proclaimed a proud accomplishment with an under 3.0% increase in municipal taxes---but there were no newly funded actions to help the community become more resilient and the set-aside amount of $426,000 in a climate change fund amounted to .0015% of the City's $292.7 million operating budget. No climate emergency plan was in sight at this writing so very little had changed. Further, the City of Peterborough's own budget process included a survey that ranked the top 12 categories of focus of concern from its own citizens. Climate change ranked fourth; however, all of the other categories are likely to be negatively impacted if the first priority doesn't change soon to the vision and mission of building community resilience as the integrated response to the climate emergency.

Based on my business experience, I recognized budgets of this magnitude as the financial support to specific plans that supported moving closer to a Vision.

The problem to me is that the City has repeatedly demonstrated the total lack of a vision with supporting goals and any specific plans to support it. Generally speaking, with no vision it's very difficult to progress by any measure either for a city or a business.

I need to admit upfront that I have extreme difficulty with the celebration of the finalization of a 2021 budget, no matter how hard it was to balance because of COVID-19, that holds the property tax increase to a predetermined figure of under 3%. This is not the first City of Peterborough budget that disappointed me; however, it is the first of such budgets after the declaration by City Council of a climate emergency. I expected more.

It's worth noting that the City and County of Peterborough and First Nations have all approved a Sustainable Peterborough Plan (SPP) and a Climate Change Action Plan (CCAP) prepared by outside consultants at a total cost of close to a million dollars. Both plans received much community support, including from TTP, but close to zero financial support over the past ten years from the City and County. Both are seemingly political documents allowing the City and County to share in the gas tax. But contrary to what the public seems to think, the gas-tax money does not flow directly into climate emergency mitigation or adaptation projects.

On a positive note, after our consultation with one City councillor, she did suggest to the City treasurer that he invite TTP to make a formal presentation to the City of Peterborough with respect to the use of the funds from the sale of the City-owned power distribution company known as PDI. That proposal, titled "Renewable Power Generation Investment Trust Fund" is shown in Chapter 3 along with a follow-up letter to the sub-committee of Council, called the PDI Investment Options Working Group, charged with making a recommendation to City Council as a whole. The TTP proposal was one of six proposals made. As of this date, no decision on this proposal has been made public. That decision may be made before the completion of this book. If so, it will be reported herein.

As an added note, TTP, as a member of the Save PDI Citizens Coalition, was part of the opposition to the sale of PDI to Hydro One. By survey, the sale of PDI to Hydro One was opposed by over 90% of the citizens served by the City-owned PDI power distribution company.

CHAPTER 2
POST CARBON CHATTER

FOREWARD, DECEMBER 2020

Multiple countries around the world and big global businesses are jumping on the bandwagon to announce their goals to be zero-carbon by 2050. Certainly, we need goals, but so often these goals are not backed up by realistic plans or any financial commitment to achieve them. To be carbon-free by 2050 as a global business is one thing, albeit highly suspect, but for an entire country or the world--- ? Whoever is selling this is likely also selling swampland in Florida before such land totally disappears from rising sea levels. We are addicted to fossil fuels, and we simply will not be able to kick the habit by 2050--- unless we are forced to with a total collapse!

This is where building human-scale community resilience comes in. Much more of that as we proceed. For now, let's talk about energy.

Amazon, the largest company in the world by market capitalization has already announced its goal to be carbon-free by 2050 with its entire fleet of trucks slated to be electrically powered by renewable energy. This is really great public relations (PR) and likely good for the planet, but we need to be realistic. It doesn't mean that all of Amazon's electric delivery trucks and drones, powered by solar or wind or other renewable sources of energy will not utilize enormous amounts of oil and rare earths in their discovery and manufacture. There is no sign yet that we can build electric cars, solar panels, or huge wind turbines to a global scale without using enormous amounts of oil; and we certainly can't rebuild the total global fleet of hydroelectric dams and nuclear power plants without oil.

Consumerism, representing about seventy percent of Western economies such as Canada's, has duped us into totally ignoring our life essentials. Energy is certainly one of the key life essentials that more than ever in human history has been taken for granted. Few of us recognize the enormous amount of energy in a barrel of oil or the amazing amount of excess energy required to run the global complex society in which we live. And no one knows how much energy is required to move the internet to 5G and for Jeremy Rifkin's *Internet of Things (IoT)* and *The Third Industrial Revolution*, let alone if the benefits of the technology they represent will be affordable enough to be widely available to the masses.

This doesn't mean that some of the new technology will not be required to transition from where we are now to a new more resilient place. What we do have to understand is that we are at the point of societal complexity whereby every increase in complexity also increases our collective vulnerability and has a marginal return in our quality of life by any measure.

And for good measure, as already stated, we haven't figured out as a global society just exactly what source of renewable energy can replace oil to rebuild aging solar panels, windmills or even nuclear power plants. Nuclear fusion, not fission, may well be the future of the human race, but it will take one hell of a lot of fossil fuels to even answer the feasibility question, let alone build out to a global scale.

Fortunately, the Transition Towns movement has always understood that without a significant amount of net energy descent there would be no way for the entire global population to live in such a complex society without the benefit of oil. The best we can do is to focus on reducing the amount of oil we consume per capita and build community resilience in those communities that have some chance of being re-designed to human scale and sustained at that level long enough to bridge to a new way of life that can endure the ravages of what lies ahead. Peterborough, Ontario, is one such town.

The TNP is an energy descent initiative. Despite our many local communications efforts on this and other related topics about oil and our economy, most of the world's population believes that all we need do is switch to renewable energy and everything will fall into place. We will drive electric cars and driver-less electric cabs will be at every corner in our bigger cities. Drones overhead will deliver ever-larger packages to our front door, and a regenerative countryside in smaller towns like Peterborough, existing in harmony with nature, will provide the connection to our soul for weekend retreats.

Remember that English TV series of ten years ago called *Escape to the Country*. The rich moved to the countryside to get away from the madness of the City of London and other larger cities in England. These wonderful folks, as portrayed on the TV show, drove up all the housing prices in the nearby quaint little villages, just as the Torontonians are doing coming to Peterborough and the other small towns along Lake Ontario bringing with them a chronic need for affordable housing for those citizens who have been marginalized and certainly in Peterborough making it much more difficult for new family formation and home ownership.

These words are hopefully and not mysteriously in support of the fundamental Transition Towns idea that the way we will be able to live in the future is mostly about life's essentials, namely our food, water, energy, wellness and culture--- one community at a time.

At this time, on the energy front at least, there is little opportunity for the Greater Peterborough Area to become free of fossil fuels by 2050, basically because we are trending towards becoming a bedroom community of the Oshawa area which is, in turn, a bedroom community of Toronto east of Yonge St. as planned by provincial governments of all political persuasions dedicated to supporting cars no matter the cost and not capable of understanding the need for life at human scale.

However, what is possible on energy in Peterborough is for the community to become a net-positive renewable energy community by 2035. While not free of all fossil fuels, the community would be generating more renewable energy locally in total than it consumes of all types of energy in total, including the electricity from nuclear power, hydro and fossil fuels. This means that if the very fragile local grid now owned by Hydro One were wired to keep all of the energy generated here in the area for its own consumption the city could cover its own needs and actually have an excess amount of energy to feed into the grid for use outside the community. This is based on the distributive power model where most of the power generation occurs close to where it is consumed saving all that loss of energy in transmission, which is estimated variously at around 10%. This model and opportunity are explored further in this book.

The international classification of nuclear- and hydro-sourced electricity as green energy is political balderdash and ignores the enormous amount of embedded fossil fuels required to build them, maintain and eventually refurbish and replace them.

Needless to say, the Peterborough area because of its relatively small size and location surrounded by a mix of farmland and green space has a much greater opportunity than Oshawa or Toronto to become a net-positive renewable energy community.

This second chapter presents a series of articles that I have written in the past that I believe are necessary to have some appreciation for the need to help our society towards building resilience to the long emergency that lies ahead. I do wish to use the verbiage "the long emergency" because that is what it is and if we don't take it very seriously, we are doomed as a species. Further, I wish to recognize the work of James Howard Kunstler who published his book titled *The Long Emergency in*

2005 and a follow-up book titled *Living in the Long Emergency* published this year, 2020.

What this book, in aggregate attempts to put forward, is a way for the citizens of the Greater Peterborough Community in Ontario, Canada, of approximately 121,000 people and growing can celebrate living in the Long Emergency with some level of shared resilience, prosperity and vitality.

OUR CASINO ECONOMY:
Gambling against the House for a Better Life
(as published in *Greenzine* magazine in 2016)

When the entire population of North America, minus the elite 1%, line up to buy a billion-dollar lottery ticket, we will recognize our casino economy in full force--- a probable outcome of an unsustainable economic system where most of us are gambling against the house for a better life.

John Michael Greer writes of three distinct economies in his book *The Wealth of Nature: Economics as if Survival Mattered*. The natural economy provides nature's services, including trees, soil, minerals, marine life, animals, water, the air we breathe and, most certainly, the energy from fossil fuels that have powered the secondary economy from the beginning of the Industrial Revolution.

The secondary economy is human-made and is the one that for most of the time in our economic history has produced the vast array of goods and services that bring us good health, long life, happiness and prosperity. To give you some idea of how dependent the secondary economy, which for most of us is indeed the REAL economy, is dependent on the bounty of our natural economy, we reference Robert Costanza. In "The value of the world's ecosystems services and natural capital," as written in *Wealth of Nature* in 1997, Costanza suggests:

> *"Out of every dollar of value circulating in the world's human economies something like 75 cents was provided by natural*

processes rather than human labour. What's more, most if not all of that 75 cents of value had to be there in advance for the production of the other 25 cents to be possible at all".

Oil is one of the natural processes.

The part that didn't need to be there before the secondary economy could generate wealth is basically the seed for the growth of the casino economy we are now living in. John Michael Greer calls this the tertiary economy--- fundamentally making money off money---put simply it's gambling often with other peoples' money by governments, the big banks, stock markets and big corporations everywhere on earth. Most often, the cards are stacked in favour of the house, owned by the elite 1%. Life in our existing casino economy for ordinary folks is like gambling against the house. And the house always wins in the end. It explains why many people living in Toronto, London, New York and the like thrive in the casino economy while producing minimum goods and services in the secondary economy. They routinely transfer the wealth from smaller communities at an ever-increasing rate and bankrupt locally owned businesses in the process in favour of big globally branded corporations.

Lottery tickets purchased mostly by the already in debt poor and middle class, with the hope of someday striking it rich, are a boom to the existing casino economy. Lotteries produce almost no useful goods or services while sucking large amounts of money from communities and putting it in the hands of the elite 1% without recourse--- It's a sham or more politically correct a tax on the poor and middle class perpetuated by governments and lobbyists to help keep the casino economy culture and reality the 21st-century economic norm.

But rather, again, from that article in *Wealth of Nature* it has to be noted:

"The three economies and the three kinds of wealth they produce are not interchangeable. Trillions of dollars in credit swaps and derivatives will not keep people from starving in the

streets if there's no food being grown and no housing being built
or maintained or offered for sale or rent."

In the overall economy, investment capital flows to the greatest return for the lowest risk. Right now and fundamentally since the mid-1970s that has been away from the secondary economy for the production of goods and services into the casino economy serving the elite 1%.

This trend has forced the labour productivity metric onto the secondary economy leading to the rise of greater automation and robotics and the overall loss of jobs. This could have been a good thing if, somehow, we were able to price into our economics the external costs of energy usage and the destructive costs to our social being and the environment caused by pollution and emissions. It just hasn't happened; so the casino economy keeps middle-class wages down, reduces the total number of jobs and causes capital migration to the lowest-cost labour alongside greater automation. Damn the environment and the inefficient use of cheap energy! Enter the climate crisis as the issue of our time. Need we connect more of the dots!

Although the concentration of wealth is far greater in most of Europe and the US, it is growing here in Canada. When both income and assets are concentrated in very few hands, such as in the 1%, the likely long-term outcome, if it is allowed to continue, is the loss of jobs and social unrest, followed by social disorder, then democratic institutional breakdown as we are now witnessing in real-time in the US and, finally, social and economic collapse. After that, no one knows what will happen. Include the immigration crisis in Europe and the US, themselves escaping from social and economic collapse in their own countries, and you already have the kind of social unrest we are now witnessing.

The only good news is that the global casino economy is most certainly slowing down along with a contracting global secondary economy with the peaking of the production of low-cost conventional oil used to drive the global economy. However, the casino economy, no matter what we do, will live on for many years, hopefully with less impact on our daily lives. That's the best we can hope for in view of the massive manipulations available to key partners in the house represented by the World Bank, the International Monetary Fund and the central banks around the world led by the US Federal Reserve.

IT'S OIL, STUPID!
(as published in *Greenzine* magazine in 2017)

It's oil that makes the world go round! It's not money. I wish it were love, but we are dreaming on that score as well. Remember when James Carville, advising Bill Clinton in his first presidential campaign, coined the phrase "It's the economy, stupid!" Well, our post–industrial modern lifestyle is still about the economy. However, now we know that our complex global capitalistic system that we call our economy runs on energy, and mostly fossil fuels. And it is the inexpensive, energy-packed, and transportable oil that fuels our cars, trucks, airplanes, freighters and pleasure ships that has made possible the globalization of trade, corporate capitalism and the casino economy in which we now live.

The global energy crisis, climate change and global economic instability are all outcomes of our total reliance on oil. We have become slaves to the very oil that has created our modern lifestyles. Most of us know of oil's impact on emissions leading to climate change. What is less understood is oil's impact on our global economy and how that is affecting the fight against climate change.

We now understand that the global economy will collapse without oil. Most economists have now caught on to the reality that when oil sells for above $100 US a barrel for a prolonged period of time Big Oil tends to make a lot of money--- the energy sector thrives and the rest of the economy tanks.

Richard Heinberg puts it this way: *"When prices are high enough to generate profits (which is very high indeed these days), they are also high enough to destroy demand."*

Now that oil prices have been down to US $40 to US $75 for a fairly long period of time, we would expect the oil producers and oil-producing countries to be less profitable and prosperous while the global economy would rebound. Certainly, profits for Big Oil and oil-producing countries are down, and bankruptcies by fracking producers, mostly in the US, are mounting fast; but the global economy in 2017 is just beginning to rebound from the global recession of 2008/09. On the whole, the Great Recession was attributed to the US subprime mortgage crisis. And the recessionary fix was all economic patchwork introducing fiscal stimulants, corporate bailouts, quantitative easing and lower interest rates, while the vital role of oil in our economic system was swept aside. Economic recovery in many countries has been either anemic or negative, begging the question of what's going on in oil?

Here are my views: Big Oil, big banks and consumers have taken on huge amounts of debt directly and indirectly to extract unconventional oil from the deep sea, Arctic, fracking shale, and Canada's tar sands while the cost of that extraction keeps on rising regardless of the market price of a barrel of oil. One of the big reasons for the rising costs is the rising amount of energy, including oil required to extract a barrel of oil. So, not only is the return on investment in dollar terms declining rapidly, but the same thing is also happening with respect to the return on energy invested.

Regardless of price, if it takes more energy to produce a barrel of oil than is in the barrel of oil, the return is negative, and that source of oil would need to eventually be shut down. Some of the unconventional sources of oil are approaching this thermodynamic limit. A reminder is in order--- our complex global economy doesn't actually run on the oil produced that we hear about in the news, but rather on the excess amount of oil that remains after we subtract the amount of oil and other forms of energy required to produce that oil--- this is called "excess energy." This is what has made globalization, the internet, and all of the plastic and other products we routinely rely on in our everyday lives. But the amount of excess oil to run the global economy is in sharp decline, causing the real global economy to move into contraction.

Further, when the market price of oil declines, as we see now as a result of a supply bubble, the financial return is not sufficient to pay the interest on the debt accumulated to extract that oil. That's fairly well understood --- what is not is the drag on the overall economy created by that debt. Specifically, much less money is available to invest in green energy technologies to help reduce climate change--- even when the financial returns are higher.

So, we are in a Catch-22. The rising cost of extraction has caused a debt bubble that we can't afford to pay off without global economic growth while the amount of excess energy from oil required to grow the total economy is in sharp decline; this is causing an economic contraction in the real economy on Main Street for ordinary folks everywhere. No plan exists to allocate global oil to provide life essentials, such as food, water, energy, wellness and culture to the masses, balanced with the need to switch to more sustainable sources of energy and lifestyles that use a lot less of the stuff.

Communities all over the world are left to fare for themselves and build their own economic localization infrastructure and conserve all forms of energy.

Predictably, the next recession will be more devastating than the last and will be blamed on the debt bubble and the lack of economic growth to support that debt, both public and private. Jobs will disappear like they never have before and the investment funds required to fight climate change may well dry up, setting back mitigation and adaptation another ten years. However, the root cause of the recession will again be what has been going on with global oil. It's oil, stupid!

THE FOX AND THE HARE
(as published in *Greenzine* magazine 2015)

If the fox consumes more energy hunting for and chasing the hare than he gets from eating the hare, the fox eventually dies.

Because the climate crisis that we now face in our daily lives is in reality an energy crisis, we offer the the fox and the hare as a clear representation of the most important laws of nature that govern the lives of all living things, especially now with respect to our human existence in the complex civilization we have created since the First Industrial Revolution.

The three laws are:

Energy can neither be created nor destroyed: it can only be transformed--- The fox transforms the food energy stored in the hare to its own body energy storage system.

Entropy: leads to a loss of some energy in every transformation of energy---The fox loses some part of the energy stored in the hare in the act of preparing its meal for consumption and in the actual act of consumption.

All energy in all its forms that exist on earth originates from the sun: The fox is a representation of a transformation of energy from the sun, as are we humans and every other plant or animal species on the planet.

From these basic laws, we have grown to understand that all fossil fuels are ancient sunlight. Our modern complex society began when we started to exploit the energy stored from ancient sunlight in the form of fossil fuels starting with coal firing the early steam engines. Ancient sunlight in the form of fossil fuels is a finite resource requiring more and more fossil fuels to actually discover and process them into usable forms, such as gasoline, jet fuel and diesel fuel used in our transportation systems.

As a practical matter, when we consume more energy to discover and process an energy source within the safety limits of pollution of our human existence than we get by using it, then we have a negative return on our energy. This is expressed as energy return on energy invested (EROEI). In the case of the fox in this situation, he dies. In the case of our modern civilization, we can keep printing money and throwing it into the mix with negative return on investment (ROI) until the debt bubble bursts and the economic system crashes. This is exactly what is happening now with reference to the Canadian tar sands and the US fracking oil & gas industry. We are pumping more and more money into the production of oil to keep our economy growing with very little and often negative ROI.

Another frightening story about the food energy we humans consume is that our industrial food supply consumes far more energy than we humans gain by eating that food, creating a food-waste bubble across the planet on land and in the oceans that is leading directly to the extinction of many other plant and animal species. Sourcing much more of our own food locally is part of the great transformation to a post-carbon economy in Peterborough.

I need to re-emphasize a few points that I have already touched on. Firstly, our complex civilization runs on excess energy from ancient sunlight including fossil fuels, geothermal and atomic. Secondly, all of these forms of energy are in sharp decline at any cost to discover, extract and process. These two factors lead us to the stark reality that we cannot continue to support our complex civilization for the masses, which include all but the elite 1%, by simply switching to renewable forms of energy. The new post-carbon economy will have to be preceded by a net per capita energy descent to carry on with any society that in fundamental ways resembles our current lifestyles. This reality leads directly to the Resiliency Imperative.

WHAT ENERGY CRISIS!
(as published in *Greenzine* magazine in 2015)

We are not running out of energy. Scientists inform us that energy cannot be created or destroyed, it can only be transformed. In fact, the fundamental living, breathing planetary process is the conversion of our sun's energy to grow vegetation, thereby providing the food energy for all species, including humans, to continue their magical energy transformational life processes.

All living populations grow with an excess supply of food energy. This goes for plants and animals, including foxes, tigers, bears, insects, whales, elephants and humans. And when predators are non-existing or declining, populations can grow exponentially to their environmental limit.

We, humans, are at the top of the food chain and are a predator of all living things on planet earth. And we have no natural predator save the limitations enforced by Mother Earth. We directly or indirectly consume all other species of plants and animals in massive energy conversion to feed ourselves. Is it any wonder that we are pushing our planetary limit with seven billion hungry people. Past civilizations have collapsed as they reached their own environmental limit for access to food energy.

Most of us have heard the expression that we are what we eat. There is amazing truth in that statement. And what we have been eating since the start of the industrial revolution is fossil fuels, directly and indirectly. There is no escaping it. Follow the oil, not the money, through our complex civilization to verify this reality. Our earth was reasonably balanced for vast diversity of life on land and our oceans before the Industrial Revolution. The Industrial Revolution did not cause the human population explosion, but the fossil fuels that fired the revolution certainly did: first with coal, followed by natural gas and oil. These fossil fuels are what we humans have been eating ever since in ever-increasing amounts at accelerated rates. In fossil fuels, we have huge amounts of energy, known as ancient sunlight, that is compact and easily transportable, so much so that we have developed robotic cars to take us anywhere on land and even robotic airplanes and rockets to the moon to dream impossible dreams of interplanetary space travel to escape our polluted oasis.

The predicaments caused by our unrelenting burning consumption of fossil fuels seem to have escaped most of our populace. The energy crisis itself is driving climate change, global pollution, on land, in our air and in our oceans, and global economic contraction. With little understanding of the energy crisis, our civilization and our species face a very uncertain future.

THE BURSTING CARBON BUBBLE
(as published in *Greenzine* magazine in 2019)

The carbon bubble isn't about to burst--- it already has!

But the worst is yet to come, and we are being lulled into a new but lower level of economic comfort with low oil and gas prices and deals on gas-guzzling cars and trucks.

My concern is that we seem to be suppressing any effort to understand the bursting carbon bubble to save ourselves and our communities from the likely devastating economic impact of it while mitigating the most life-changing negative effects of climate change.

With Trump in the White House and an America First economic policy, it appears that the top three oil-producing nations, Russia, Saudi Arabia and the US, are in some kind of cartel to continue to flood the market with cheap oil, leaving the smaller producers forced to face economic collapse even before the forces of climate change demand that the remaining oil stay in the ground.

It's already apparent that some elite private investors within the big three oil-producing nations and around the world are divesting from oil to protect their personal fortunes--- while denying climate change and actually encouraging the masses to keep on consuming fossil fuels.

Many coal-producing companies are insolvent and even the big global oil companies, while having the highest profits in their history, are dealing with early signs of insolvency.

It's not a conspiracy theory surmising what might happen to individual citizens economically when the big carbon burst arrives, but rather a well-founded observation of the lack of interest and understanding by ordinary citizens of how critical fossil fuels are to sustaining our modern technocratic consumer-driven lifestyle and the pressing need to protect their assets and career choices from the bursting carbon bubble.

The carbon bubble began to burst just after the price of oil rising to $147 US precipitated the US subprime mortgage crisis. Thousands of people were forced to choose between paying for their food and gas to go to work or paying their mortgage. This led to the global Great Recession of 2008/09 from which millions of people around the world and many sovereign states have not recovered.

There was no advance warning by the Wall St. elite to the unknowing masses of the enormous risk they were taking in the bundling of subprime mortgages, and as it turned out neither Wall St. nor the billionaire class paid the price--- it was the rest of us.

As of November 2016, the Paris COP 21 Climate Change Agreement became binding with almost all nations of the world, including the US and Canada, signing on and committing to keep the average global temperature rise to no more than 2°C.

This agreement serves as the marker of the really big bursting carbon bubble.

Why? Because most climatologists now advocate that to have any chance of holding global temperature rise to 2°C, up to 80% of all the coal, natural gas and oil reserves on earth must stay in the ground.

Although the 80% figure seems aspirational at best, the Paris Agreement has pushed the global discussion on how to reduce emissions into high gear and far beyond carbon taxes or cap and trade.

Notwithstanding the global trend to localism to reduce energy consumption and carbon emissions, the big carbon bubble burst is arguably more likely to happen in our casino economy when investors in major fossil fuel assets begin to assess the risk in holding these assets.

Despite the clean coal charade, the jury is already in on coal, the dirtiest fossil fuel; however, both oil and natural gas are getting what amounts to free passage because of their very successful lobbying against climate change.

Significantly, Michael Bloomberg, former mayor of New York City and chair of the non-profit Sustainable Accounting Standards, has begun efforts to create standards industry by industry for companies to disclose climate change risk on their annual financial statements. And Black Rock, the world's largest asset manager with total assets nearing $5 trillion, issued a report in September 2016 recommending investors include climate risks in their decisions.

Predictably, when the risk assessment guidelines are in full force across industries from airlines to gas and oil to transportation to coastal housing, the cost of capital will certainly rise for climate risk investments and the big carbon bubble burst will be apparent to everyone.

The question is who will pay the price for all the climate-change-stranded assets?

Will it be the elite 1% or will it be the rest of us one way or another?

Welcome to the world of localism.

BOLD & LOCAL ECONOMIC INFRASTRUCTURE:
The Antidote to Global Capitalism and the Climate Crisis
(as published in *Greenzine* magazine in 2019)

It is now well-documented and broadly understood that global corporate capitalism is driving rampant consumerism and the global climate crisis. This entrenched capitalism continues to suck much of the capital out of local communities literally putting it into the pockets of the already rich. You can hear the sound of this monetary-sucking noise through large plastic straws that we no longer need.

(handwritten note in top margin)

If you live in Peterborough, I invite you to stand outside Costco or Walmart or any of the other big-box retailers and try to visualize how much of the money spent inside these stores ever comes back in support of our local economy. I won't bore you with the facts, but these stores don't create jobs; they destroy jobs in our community. If you want to continue to live in the community, you also ought to think of where you spend your money so that you and your children and your neighbours and their children get to keep their jobs.

Rare is the local community that has escaped the wrath of job loss and vitality to global capitalism, and rare is the community that thinks it has enough remaining capital to revitalize its own local economy ... but pull ourselves up by our own economic bootstraps we must.

The antidote to the economic mess we are now in is bold community-level economic localization infrastructure. Examples of such infrastructure abound, such as: special economic zones, local currencies, local foundations, local investment funds, local public trusts, local utilities investing in energy descent and local power generation, local energy and food co-ops and public banks that leverage municipal reserves into new capital formation for local investment.

We don't exactly know when globalization will begin its long descent, but there are signs that it is plateauing as many more global citizens face the stark reality that the climate crisis is a real and present danger and that we humans are responsible for dramatically overshooting the carrying capacity of our planet on every front imaginable.

The antidote is clearly for a large portion of the global population to live more locally.

Facing this reality as individuals and families is the first step.

The second step is to rebuild the economic infrastructure that supports living more locally and dramatically cuts our carbon footprint.

This second step may be even more difficult than the first because it involves our local governments joining with their own citizens in support of locally owned businesses and local farming enterprises that create jobs that support a more vital and prosperous community.

It's especially difficult because in 2019 most of us residing in Peterborough don't actually live here very much anymore. We mostly live in the global universe, on the internet, with the TV streaming our major source of entertainment, and at the front door receiving packages from a faceless company called Amazon. Because we don't live here very much, it becomes very difficult to get us all together thinking about how we might change the way we live and help to mitigate and adapt to the worst effects of the climate change crisis.

But that is precisely the mission of Transition Town Peterborough and all of its initiatives including the Kawartha Loon local currency, Transition Neighbourhoods Project, Purple Onion Harvest Festival, Dandelion Day Festival, Local Food Month, ResilientPtbo 2030 and the *Greenzine* magazine with "Building Our Local Living Economy" as its enduring tag line now moving into its 12th year in 2020.

GLOBAL FIRE, LOCAL GEM

(as published in *Greenzine* magazine in 2018)

Globalization is a result of cheap energy and corporate capitalism chasing the lowest cost of labour wherever it is anywhere on the globe--- all with the bulk of the reward (profit) going to the already rich. The already rich are invested in the Global FIRE (finance, insurance and real estate) sector which drives the entire global economy. What we aren't yet prepared to face is that the globalization of our economics has also globalized much of our social capital, social localism and sense of place and identity. That is the struggle we face as a community in the face of the climate crisis.

Returning to the economy as the driver of change---there is no such thing as a free competitive market--- there are a bunch of rules and policies made with governments, the FIRE lobby, and trade deals that have locked in the advantage that globalization has over local economies. The FIRE sector, which comprises finance, including the privatized banking system that creates all our money allowing the monetization of just about everything on earth, and insurance and real estate, is where our money is... including the money of the well-off folks who live in Peterborough. Very little of the capital accumulation of Peterborough residents remain here to re-circulate in the local economy creating new wealth and new local sustainable jobs. We need to tap into that local wealth to give us the needed boost to localize much more of our economy. The trick is to design attractive investment infrastructure to support economic localization. Putting it rather bluntly, there are a fair number of well-off people living in the Greater Peterborough Area (GPA) but many of them are not invested here---their capital is invested in the global economy.

In Peterborough, the FIRE economy is very small, certainly compared to Toronto, the so-called financial capital of Canada. The real estate portion of the FIRE economy is far larger in importance in Toronto as compared to Peterborough. Torontonians are far more interested in the bursting of the real estate bubble than they are the carbon bubble.

The largest employment sector and likely the largest economic driver in Peterborough is the GEM sector, which stands for government, education and medical. Without this sector, Peterborough would be well on its way to becoming a hollowed-out bedroom community and a place to retire after years of hard work in the big city.

The opportunity for Peterborough comes down to how do we keep more of the money generated here re-circulating through investment and spending in our community for the security, happiness and well-being of local citizens. In financial language, how do we build the economic localization infrastructure that potentially localizes half our economy leading with life essentials---food, water, energy, wellness, and culture---indeed the mission of Transition Town Peterborough.

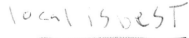

LIVING LOCALLY:
Harnessing the Power of Our Citizens
(as published in *Greenzine* magazine in 2015)

Organize your home to live more locally and you'll be doing as much economic development for Peterborough as any job creation program. That may seem like a bold statement to many of us now excited yet enslaved by the internet and the seemingly unending progress of technology and globalization.

The critical point is that we need to live locally---breathe local air, drink local water, eat local food, utilize local energy, maintain our health with local provisions and engage in local culture and entertainment---within the bubble of technology and globalization no matter its promise.

Most of us live physically in the Peterborough area. We breathe local air, drink local water but after that, we've put our lives in the hands of globalization and corporate capitalism. We know about the latest Apple device and the terrorist attack in Australia within minutes, but we don't know where our food comes from. Our industrial food is so highly processed with salt, sugar and unhealthy fats that it has become the major cause of the killer diseases of our time: obesity, cancer, high blood pressure, and heart. Not coincidentally, these diseases are the major cause of rising health care costs and the run-up of our Ontario sovereign debt that is sure to burden the lives of our children and grandchildren.

Capitalism was never designed to be fair.

Capitalism itself, anchored in the idea of continuous economic growth, was never designed to be fair to all of us. We have been brainwashed by economists, the media, big businesses and governments to believe that continuous economic growth will lift everyone and is, therefore, the road to increased social justice and poverty reduction everywhere. Until the late 1970s or so, there were elements of truth in this *"raise all boats"* economic theory. Then the boat sprang leaks with the switch from internationalism to globalization with abundant cheap oil to provide the energy for increased free trade and globalization, a focus on the lowest cost of labour, and finally corporate capitalism's takeover of Western economic and political systems, ultimately even Communist China. During the same time, the debate of democracy-versus-socialism has been muted by corporate capitalism now dominating the social order of both systems.

This all happened with global corporations' clear pursuit of one thing and one thing only---profit. It's all about money. Global corporations will roll over everything, including political borders and people to make more money and indeed more money on money. Enter a new level of parasitic control by big banks and the big bondholders. Bottom line: corporate capitalism is not about bettering people's lives and now not even about the products and services that are designed to serve people in the real economy. It's about making money, lots of it, with most of it making the already rich, super-rich.

Thirty-five years of corporate capitalism and globalization have brought us to our knees.

The result of 35 years of corporate capitalism and globalization has devastated local communities with a gradual but accelerating disintegration of social justice and the very premise of the western liberal democracies originally designed to serve the best interests of their people.

Now, in 2015, at the peak of the global corporate capitalism that has brought us to our knees, we face governments in Canada at the federal, provincial and local level that remain committed to that style of capitalism fostering continuous economic growth at all cost as the one and only solution to all of our problems. Anything getting in the way of this long-broken theoretical economic system is pushed aside with incredible certitude.

Continuing along the path of corporate capitalism and globalization is insane!

The broken global corporate capitalistic system is oddly trying to reboot with both austerity and stimulus and certainly with heightened support for consumerism, more imports from free trade deals and the likes of Black Friday. Now we have heightened competition between oil-producing nations for market share and no one, least of all economists, can forecast the outcome of this global game of economic roulette.

It's frightening and not the least bit sustainable. However, sustainability itself has been successfully green washed by big banks, Big Oil and governments, so there is not much point in making that point over and over again. To gain some attention to what is really happening, let's call it what it is---**insane!**

Where is the money coming from to localize our economy so we can live locally?

Peterborough Economic Development (PED) Corporation's Five-Year Strategic Plan released in 2014, and written with taxpayers' money, says, *"In order to succeed, we must tap into, engage and harness the power of the people of our community to become active economic champions and ambassadors."* This is a marvelous statement, supportive of Transition Town's strategic direction and the transition initiatives that support living locally. However, it is something much less than a plan to help make it happen, especially in view of the strategic plan's narrative setting out the all-important fact that PED is operating in a *"resource-constrained environment."* That's code for it's not going to happen without a lot more money. A similarly supportive statement noting the need for financing was made by Tom Phillips, Trent University economics professor, in the summary paragraph of his "Building on Peterborough's new tech success" article published in the *Examiner* in December 2014:

> *"With the right supports, encouragement, and financing, we could use the substantial resources and expertise that we now*

have in our community to ensure its prosperity for the coming generation. That is a legacy that my parents' generation would be proud of."

What we have is our Peterborough Economic Development Corporation and one of our most prominent local economists seeing a bright shining light for future community prosperity, but only musing as to where the money will come from to make it happen.

The short answer on the money issue to re-build the local economy is that much if not most of the money is going to have to come from the local taxpayer. We can't expect corporate capitalism, including big banks and Big Oil, to bail out our local economy. They are all too happy to continue sucking money out of the community. The federal government is not inclined and is hard on the destructive path of oil development and economic growth. The provincial government has big plans for green energy and even local food but little money to support them or for local economic development zones.

And so, it comes down to the local municipal government. Unfortunately, its mandate is perceived such as to avoid the responsibility to help build the local economic infrastructure to harness our own citizens' abilities to invent a future of greater prosperity and social justice. Should we build new roads and sports complexes while ignoring the cost to rebuild our local economic infrastructure so our people can make a living? Which comes first? Shouldn't the City and County prioritize the need for millions of dollars over the next ten years for economic infrastructure development?

That bright shining light is the New Economy.

The new economy is what the Peterborough Economic Development Corporation, Professor Tom Phillips and Transition Town are talking about. It marries the so-called creative class with localized economic development to not only create a more vibrant, resilient and prosperous community but one with a much lower and sustainable carbon footprint.

The new economy focuses on solutions rooted in our shared values of entrepreneurship, democracy, transparency, accountability, inclusiveness and diversity. It harnesses the power of our community and extends social justice.

Living Locally is a critical component of the New Economy.

The transition town "Living Locally" movement counterbalances corporate capitalism and globalization. It's not about replacing all the products of globalization. We know that we aren't going to make cars or TV sets any time soon in Peterborough. What it is about is increasing community resilience through economic localization of life essential goods and services. It's a critical component of the bright shining light more people are starting to see. It is the new economy.

The real change is one of lifestyle and values. It is the move from local but global consumers into responsible citizens who understand their own power and the power of buying locally and living locally. We say "responsible citizens" in the sense that we understand the trade-off of price versus value, that shopping at local big-box retailers may be buying local, but it isn't living locally.

Living Locally means a lot of things socially, environmentally and politically. Economically, living locally means sourcing most of everything we need in terms of products and services from local farmers and locally owned businesses.

If enough of us live locally we begin to harness the power of our people to take back control of our lives and a much bigger part of our economy---the local economy.

Transition Town initiatives demonstrate the New Economy.

Transition Town initiatives, including the Kawartha Loon local currency, this *Greenzine* publication, the Purple Onion Festival, Dandelion Day,

kawarthaLoon prog.t
get done

Loonie Saturdays, the Transition Skills Forum, the Public Trust Proposal for Economic Localization Infrastructure Development and the 25% Shift Local Food Peterborough are designed to support economic localization. They are economic development demonstration initiatives of living more locally and how citizens can harness their power to do so.

The promise of living more locally is now well-documented in terms of reducing our carbon footprint, improving social justice and creating a more prosperous, vital economy that creates more sustainable jobs and livelihoods.

You are invited to become a local economic development ambassador. Live locally. Shop with the Kawartha Loon local currency at locally owned businesses and farming enterprises.

Harness your power as a citizen of your community!

LOCAL FOOD SECURITY:
Connecting the Dots to the Climate Crisis

(as published in *Greenzine* magazine in 2019) *here unfortunate*

I must confess. I have three smart grown sons who are seemingly unable to connect the dots between their own food security and the climate crisis. For starters, they are all increasingly isolated and yet remain proud climate change deniers. How indeed does that happen? I really need your help with that!

All three of my sons believe that they eat well and with healthy food---one of them eats close to 100% organic. They all relate to their food pretty much like most Canadians--- that is they believe that we should all work hard, get an education and a good job, pay for our own food and look after ourselves. They are responsible. However, they all fail to connect even their own food security to the climate crisis and the burning of fossil fuels let alone the food security of their respective communities, all of which are in Canada.

All of my sons would understand that the abundant availability of fossil fuels has fired global population and economic growth since the First Industrial Revolution and created the mass global migration from farms to cities. They likely also know that our livestock release large amounts of methane into our atmosphere as a greenhouse gas with much greater potency than CO_2.

However, none of my sons have ever followed fossil fuel through our food system and connected it to our climate crisis. In fact, our industrial food system consumes much more energy (mostly fossil fuels) than we humans get from eating that food. We are virtually eating oil. The system is simply unsustainable as the climate crisis forces us all to think in terms of the efficient use of energy for our very own security in all aspects of our lives, including the food we eat.

"Farmers Feed Cities" is a compelling reality and yet it fails to connect that our very food security is connected to the excessive use of fossil fuels and hence to the climate crisis.

Here in Peterborough, we have formally recognized the climate crisis in the Sustainable Peterborough Plan (SPP) and the Climate Change Action Plan. The SPP even lays out the goal of Peterborough feeding ourselves by 2035. However, you can scour the City and County budgets to try to find ten cents to help make the Greater Peterborough Area more food secure. It's just not there. In reality, the City and County of Peterborough have not yet accepted any jurisdictional responsibility for local food security--- so it's all up to us citizens to lead the way.

The climate crisis demands that we think systemically and connect the dots to the energy, food and housing crises, all of which are playing out here in Peterborough in real-time.

The transition towns movement here in Peterborough and around the world was founded on the belief that our best chance to mitigate and adapt to these predicaments is to forge much stronger partnerships between local municipal governments, local not-for-profit organizations including the faith community and locally owned businesses.

We in transition continue to believe in and pursue this strategy with locally owned businesses and other non-profits but find the weakness in the strategy to be the lack of financial participation of our local municipal governments needed to kick-start and leverage the community effort as a whole.

For me, it comes down to implementing what I will call the 2% Municipal Solution to support mitigation and adaptation to the climate crisis. How to implement it? Firstly, I advocate freezing many of the budget centres at 2019 levels going into 2020 and then setting aside 1% of the operating plan in the first year for the Climate Crisis Deep Adaptation Fund. In future years, 0.1% more would be added each year until we get to 2% in 10 years.

Of course, it will soon become critical to find a low-cost means to leverage these funds and equitably distribute them throughout the community. The 2% Municipal Solution will be expanded upon in the next Climate Change Edition of *Greenzine*. In the interim please feel free to contact me at my g-mail address. We certainly need your help to present this to Council and to work on the economic impact of a more food-secure Peterborough.

2% MUNICIPAL SOLUTION:
Transitioning to a Post-Carbon Economy in Peterborough
(as published in *Greenzine* magazine in 2019)

The City of Peterborough has declared a climate emergency. What comes next! Will the County come on board and declare a similar emergency? And will the City and County come together and create a fund to support projects that reduce net energy consumption and build a much more resilient community as the foundation for the transition to a post-carbon economy by mid-century.

As defined by Richard Heinberg, *"Resilience is the capacity of a system to encounter disruption and still maintain its basic structure and function."*

That's what we want for Peterborough through to 2030. Once a fund is created, how do we plan to distribute it equitably between the City and County and between charities, not-for-profits, individuals, and for-profit locally owned businesses that can better leverage the impact more quickly at a lower cost than the City and County can do on their own?

As one example, Transition Town Peterborough has a pilot-ready homeowner energy descent initiative called the Transition Neighbourhoods Project (TNP). This project is based on behavioural economics designed to reduce the consumption of all forms of energy towards building more resilient neighbourhoods on the way to a more Resilient Peterborough. The TNP needs money from such a municipal fund as a leadership driver in this important homeowner sector.

Finally, how do we make certain that the fund expenditures are balanced systemically across the community resiliency framework of energy descent, environmental regeneration, economic localization and social and economic equity?

I have called this the "2% Municipal Fund Solution" to the climate crisis.

Nobody knows for certain what is going to happen between now and 2030 let alone by 2050 when the post-carbon economy needs to be fully functional for our very survival. So no one knows how big the fund needs to be.

The 2% figure as a percent of gross domestic product (GDP) comes from the Stern Review (2006) where it was estimated that 2% of worldwide GDP could mitigate the global climate crisis.

Thirteen years later we are now much deeper into the climate crisis, so the 2% figure is very conservative. And now we are talking less about mitigation and more about adaptation and resilience and changing our lifestyles to align with a much different world.

At the municipal level, the 2% starting figure is based on the municipal operating budgets rather than the GDP of the Peterborough Area, so it may be very conservative, but it does give us a place to start. So my recommendation is for the City of Peterborough to get started on its own with 1% of the operating plan budget in 2020, keeping within the current planned 2020 budgetary amount and committing to increase this amount by 0.1% each year through to 2030. This new fund does not take into account the capital cost of such things as the building of a regional food hub to increase our food security and cut down on food miles in our food supply chain.

I will discuss this municipal capital cost and others in future articles.

But we need to get started now!

MY LIFE STORY ON ENERGY

(as published in *Greenzine* magazine in 2017)

We Canadians are among the most favoured peoples on the planet with both an abundance of energy and water. This abundance is seemingly the root cause of the difficulty we face in accepting that we are in the midst of an energy crisis, which in itself could lead to a collapse of our way of life even before the economy craters or climate change begins to affect everything we do and our very survival.

My life story on energy started as an undergraduate in physics where I developed a deep appreciation for the work of Albert Einstein and his eloquent equation on energy $E=MC^2$. Not much of what we enjoy in our complex lifestyles would exist without Einstein and the power of his work to lead fundamental scientific research.

After undergraduate school, I worked as a lubrication engineer for Imperial Oil Ltd. Later I went on to complete an MBA in finance and marketing. By this time, energy and oil were in my DNA and shaped my worldview. This view brought clarity for me around the rise and fall of empires and ancient civilizations, the sixth extinction now well underway, the First and Second Industrial Revolutions, globalization and consumerism and the extremely comfortable but unsustainable lifestyles we enjoy in the so-called advanced Western industrialized nations.

To understand my story of energy, a basic understanding of the 1st and 2nd laws of thermodynamics is helpful. The 1st, energy can neither be created nor destroyed; the 2nd, entropy, a measure of the molecular disorder or randomness in a system. A bit of a leap from these fundamental laws leads one to appreciate that it takes energy to change energy into a form that is usable as water over a falls into electricity and fossil fuels into mechanical energy to propel cars, trains, ships and airplanes. And, further, to understand that these transformations of energy are inherently very inefficient.

Advancing a bit, we can more clearly appreciate that if some source of energy requires more energy to extract and produce than what it yields, it is an unsustainable source no matter its cost. This is the energy return on energy invested. Further, our way of life is not sustainable without a high amount of excess energy: that is, in total a high return on energy invested. Meanwhile, here we are in 2017 with total excess energy in sharp decline globally leading us all into the energy crisis whether we know about it or not. Excess energy has been covered in greater depth in previous *Greenzine* articles. One brief example---the Canadian tar sands provide a fossil fuel of very low return on energy, It takes nearly as much energy to produce a barrel of tar sands oil as the energy provided from that barrel and certainly not enough excess energy per barrel to come anywhere close to sustaining the lifestyle we have grown accustomed to.

For much of my life, I was a frustrated "Oil Peaker." I made representations after the oil embargo in the '70s on peak oil in North America. I knew about Hubbert's Curve and about CO_2 emissions and the greenhouse effect early on. I also worked internationally for the largest heating and air conditioning company in the world and was directly engaged in the ozone issue and ultimately thrilled with the nations of the world coming together with the Montreal Protocol.

I was introduced to the Transition Towns movement from an early article in the UK Ecologist magazine. This provided the missing link for me for action to mitigate and adapt to global warming... namely fossil fuels, also a program of energy descent squarely facing the energy crisis, and systems-thinking approach based on permaculture design practices and economic localization as a counterbalance to globalization for sustainable community resilience and prosperity.

In essence, the Transition Towns movement created the framework and methodology for communities to proactively mitigate and adapt as best they could, with celebration, through the converging energy crisis, climate crisis and a global capitalistic system that was failing the vast majority of people on the planet, and all of the remaining species of plants and animals. And I embraced it!

For a long time now, we have known that the only answer to the pickle we are in---let's call it the Triple-E Predicament, namely energy, environment, economy---is by very dramatic energy descent.

George Monbiot's book published in 2006, *Heat How to Stop the Planet from Burning*, in a Foreward to the Canadian Edition, calculated that Canada should cut its carbon emissions by 94% by 2030.

This number has been verified multiple times and yet ignored by virtually everyone. I suspect the number is even higher now as carbon emissions have increased since 2006. Now in 2017, we are well into the early stages of the global energy crisis with no major global energy, environmental, or economic strategy to mitigate or adapt to the new realities.

So, I can say with a high degree of confidence that the only solution to our community's need for adaptation, resilience and prosperity rests with its own citizens working together on a local basis on energy descent.

In the way of celebrating the 10th anniversary of Transition Town Peterborough, it's worth reiterating that our mission moving forward remains working together towards greater adaptation, resilience and prosperity of the community as a whole through energy descent.

Recognizing that the cliff is approaching at lightning speed.

Fred Irwin, Founding Director, Transition Town Peterborough

The following sidebar was published alongside this article:

The End of Energy Growth by Richard Heinberg, Museletter #301, June 2017

"*Dealing with the end of energy growth, and therefore economic growth is the biggest political and social challenge of our time...though it's unlikely to be recognized as such. (Our biggest ecological challenges consist of climate change, species extinctions, and ocean acidification). The impacts of the end of growth will likely be masked by financial crashes and socio-political stresses that will rivet everyone's attention while a quiet trend churns away in the background, undoing all our assumptions and expectations about the world we humans have constructed over the past couple of centuries.*

If we're smart, we will recognize that deeper trend and adapt to it in ways that preserve the best of what we have accomplished, and make life as fulfilling as it can be for as many people as possible, even while the amount of energy available to us ratchets downward. We'll act to rein in population, aim for a gradual overall population decline so that per capita energy use does not have to decline as fast as total use. We'll act to minimize ecological disruption by protecting habitat and species. We'll make happiness, not consumption, the centerpiece of economic policy.

If we are not so smart, we'll join the dinosaurs."

FOLLOW-ON COMMENTARY, END OF DECEMBER 2020:

COVID-19 hospitalizations are increasing across Canada as we move more deeply into the second wave. Thankfully, deaths as a percentage are in decline. New treatments are taking hold and multiple vaccines are on the way. The virus is far from being defeated, but we can see the light at the end of the tunnel.

From all reports and indications, Peterborough's Public Health Unit has done a remarkable job in service to our community. And we the people have diligently worn our masks, practiced social distancing, and kept our hands clean to make it happen.

However, more people are dying around the globe from the climate crisis. These numbers will, unlike from the coronavirus, keep rising for years to come if effective dramatic changes in the way we live are not implemented soon to drastically reduce carbon emissions by 2030.

And these deaths do not include the direct health effects of carbon pollution even though the evidence is mounting every day linking cancer to that pollution.

At the national level, just before Christmas, PM Justin Trudeau announced increases in the carbon tax to 2030, adding that *"recovery from the pandemic must include an ambitious climate change plan."*

Ontario's Premier Ford, reacting to Trudeau's announcement, very quickly and apparently with little knowledge of how the carbon tax actually works, is quoted that the increase in carbon tax is *"on the backs of hard-working people"* and *"the worst thing you could ever see."*

Our Peterborough Mayor Therrien is silent so far on these plans despite our official City declaration of a Climate Emergency.

As we progress further into the Climate Emergency as a community, we need to demand that at least 2% of the annual municipal operating budget be put into a climate change fund.

This will begin to harness the power of the people, the citizens of Peterborough, to leverage that money into viable initiatives such as local food security, economic localization infrastructure and renewable energy to create a more resilient Peterborough.

Email to City of Peterborough Councillor who is Chair of the Peterborough Environmental Action Committee (PEAC)

Re the 2021 Climate Change Operating Fund as announced in the amount of $426,000

December 10, 2020

1. For the longer term to 2030 we would appreciate the opportunity to input to the City how we might get this fund amount up to 2% of the operating budget by 2030. How would we go about this and in what form? Richard Freymond suggests that we work with you as the City councillor for the PEAC.

2. I may have advised you previously that we have commissioned the TCRC (Trent Community Research Centre) Research Project #4874 as attached with a working title of "Public Operating Trusts as Non-Political Economic Infrastructure for the Equitable Distribution Of Non-Capital Funds."

The TCRC project researcher is Genna Saunders.

A big advantage of the operating trust fund direction is the ability of such a trust to be non-political and supportive of long-term goals with a broad base of expertise that can bring balance to our expenditures... in transition speak, across the 4 E's System

Framework (energy, economy, environment, and equity) both social and economic.

3. Re the Short-Term Plans to Administer the $426,000 Climate Change Fund

    We understand that the motion to approve City Staff to create a report by the second quarter of 2021 will be voted on at the Council Meeting on December 14th.

    As a long-term participant in the City Project and Investment Grant Program, we would be happy to provide our input on what parts of that program could be rolled over to the climate change fund administration. The problem that the climate change fund administration will likely have stems from the lack of a City vision backed up with serious goals that promote the need for a balanced approach and expertise in renewable energy, economic localization infrastructure and local food security to name three of the critical interactive systems that are in significant need of City funding support.

    We also invited PEAC to participate with Team Transition during the pandemic to set some of the resiliency goals. Everything that Team Transition proposed appears to have fallen through the cracks and we potentially face another year lost while the climate emergency is beginning to close in on us even more.

4. Team Transition has three initiative proposals that we would like to make to the Climate Change Operating Fund Administration in 2021.

    We would appreciate your advice as to what format and timing we should utilize for these proposals. All three of these initiatives were exposed to community feedback groups before the pandemic hit.

    The first initiative is the Transition Neighbourhoods Project (TNP). This is an energy descent behavioural economics project at the household level that the City has already supported through the Investment Grant Fund.

We have now come to the pilot rolling into the full-scale implementation phase point and have no more matching funds. We were stalled out by the pandemic. It now needs to go online as well as in hard copy for starters.

We have an advisory group in place including Green Up and FRG (For Our Grandchildren) and volunteer program advisors.

The second initiative proposal is for the conversion of the Kawartha Loon local currency into a loyalty program for locally owned businesses. We will talk to PKED about partnering on this however there is little if any expertise in PKED about municipal monetary opportunities to build economic localization infrastructure creating many more jobs and livelihoods.

The third possible Team Transition initiative for 2021 is called "50% Local Food 2030." We have another TCRC project starting up in January on this topic and we know that we are completely lacking a database to develop a capital and operational funding plan for local food security. The research project is attached, #4944. We will be reaching out to PKED soon to partner with Team Transition and guide the TCRC research proposal for community input.

Your response would be most appreciated.

Best of the season,

Fred Irwin Team Transition
Transition Town Peterborough Inc.

Response to the December 10th Email:

The City councillor responded the next day via email and suggested that we work with the City infrastructure manager who is responsible for the recommendation to Council. That email was sent on the same day. We are awaiting a response from the infrastructure manager in early January 2021.

CHAPTER 3

RENEWABLE POWER GENERATION INVESTMENT TRUST FUND

CONCEPT PROPOSAL TO THE
CITY OF PETERBOROUGH
With respect to the investment of proceeds from the sale of PDI to Hydro One

Submitted by Transition Town Peterborough Inc.
171 A Rink St. Suite 166, Peterborough, On. K9J 2J6
www.transitiontownpeterborough.ca
Canada's First Transition Town

CONTENT

A. Introduction

B. Trust Fund Leading Objectives

C. Trust Fund Recommendation and Integration with the City of Peterborough's Climate Crisis Emergency Response

D. Expanding the Trust: Embracing the Whole of the City and County's Non-Capital Response to the Climate Crisis Emergency

E. Appendix A

The Resiliency Imperative & Framework: Building a More Resilient Peterborough by 2030

F. Appendix B

Resiliency Imperative & 4 E's Framework

A. Introduction

1. This Concept Proposal is presented as the first phase of a phased program planning process which includes concept/feasibility/design/implementation.

2. For reference, this concept proposal, titled "Local Renewable Power Generation Investment Trust Fund" is referenced as the **Trust Fund.**

3. The two other options as proposed to City Council are:

4. Creation of a Peterborough legacy investment fund referred to as the **Legacy Fund** and the City of Peterborough Holdings Inc. investing in renewables herein referred to as **Ptbo Holdings Fund.**

5. It is recognized that there are viable combinations of these three options that could be explored to achieve similar outcomes---some of these will be referenced in this proposal.

6. This concept proposal makes no attempt to quantify the financial return on investment and financial risk of any of the Fund Options versus the other.

7. This proposal refrains from the diversionary discussion of whether or not the City of Peterborough can actually set up an operational investment trust or structurally similar entity. That discussion and research would be part of the feasibility/design phase.

    However, Transition Town research indicates that a trust of this type can be created just as the City could set up its own municipal bank and issue its own complementary currency as Transition Town Peterborough has demonstrated. The advantages of a trust over simply a resilient community fund as an example come into play when the long-term commitment involved in the adaptation of everything to guide the City and County into the post-carbon era of 2050 is appropriately considered.

8. This proposal constitutes Transition Town Peterborough's contribution to putting the Trust Fund Option in the most favourable position to help create a more resilient community in the context of the climate crisis emergency as declared by the City of Peterborough.

9. With full disclosure Transition Town Peterborough as a not-for-profit social enterprise is not now nor an anticipated future candidate for funding from this Trust Fund Option as recommended.

B. Trust Fund Leading Objectives

Leading objectives are designed to:

- maximize the local renewable power generation of the City and County of Peterborough. The understanding is that % of energy consumed that is locally generated is a critical measure of energy security and community resilience as referenced in Appendix B.

- maximize the number of local sustainable jobs created.

- support projects that encourage local investment both large and small such as both energy co-ops and farmers' and food co-ops with energy co-op components.

- support projects that maximize the local economic multiplier effect such as those that make use of the Kawartha Loon local currency and other local supplier inputs and services.

- support the prioritization of projects that integrate renewable power generation with other life essentials including food, water, wellness and culture. These projects could include a downtown solar energy co-operative to increase energy security leading to the social and economic viability and vitality of the Peterborough downtown core as the heart and soul of the community. Other candidates for local renewable power generation systems would include the regional hospital, any local electrified public transportation system, any physical infrastructure regional food hub and year-round farmers' market, Trent University, Fleming College and any future replacement of the Memorial Centre.

- integrate with projects that also lead to and support energy descent required to make the community even more resilient.

C. Trust Fund Recommendation and Integration with the City of Peterborough's Climate Crisis Emergency Response

1. The lack of integration of any of the three options with our local climate crisis emergency response has to be considered an opportunity loss of significant magnitude. The Trust Fund recommendation is considered the best option to help move the community into a robust leadership position with respect to its Climate Crisis Emergency Response.

2. The Trust Fund Option as recommended is for a minimum of $50 million into the Trust and the balance of proceeds from the sale of PDI to be held in a short-term investment reserve to firstly set up the trust operation and executive and operating staffing to launch within a year.

3. This recommendation is presented in support of the idea that a capital gain produced by long term investment by the citizens of the City and County of Peterborough such as we have with the sale of PDI needs to be invested for the long-term energy security and the 4 E's Framework benefit of those same citizens. The 4 E's Framework is presented in the attached Appendix B.

4. The Trust Fund Option would be formed at arm's length from the City of Peterborough with likely two City councillors on the board of directors serving in an oversight capacity while productively removing politics from the investment decision-making process for greater local energy security.

5. The trust fund would be an operational investment trust with some characteristics and skill sets that are inherent in both the Legacy Fund Option and the Ptbo Holdings Option. As an example, The Trust Fund Option would likely use a commercial risk analysis and rate of return objectives such as already exist in both of the other two options. However, the Trust Fund Option would only invest in local renewable energy projects both large and small while the Legacy Fund Option would likely be shaped to maximize the return on investment (ROI) with little or no constraint on investment location or type of investment.

6. It is recognized that all or part of the return from both the Legacy Fund Option or the Ptbo Holdings Option could be re-invested in a resilient community fund. However, relying on future City Councils to keep that re-investment in place during times of budgetary constraints such as what now exists during the COVID-19 pandemic supports the need for a trust fund committed to the long-term objectives as presented in Section B.

7. The Legacy Fund represents the least desirable option with marginal opportunity to provide any more leverage against the trust fund objectives as outlined in Section B than the re-investment of the return as presented above.

8. Ptbo Holdings has very important and marketable skills involving the oversight if not the actual work to evaluate and engineer renewable energy projects of all types including integration with the existing local grid soon to be owned and operated

by Hydro One. It also has the skill to act as an operator of large- and medium-size energy projects of various types and has further demonstrated the ability to work with both commercial and residential users on increasing energy efficiency.

Unfortunately, the ability to advocate and promote energy efficiency without strong dedication to a net community-wide energy descent initiative is not likely to create the resilient community needed to flourish in the post-carbon era. Suggesting that Ptbo Holdings could maximize the community's renewable energy projects while supporting and promoting energy efficiency and then asking them to lead the drive for net community-wide energy descent is like asking them to shoot themselves in the foot and plan for their own demise. It's simply not a compatible mission for Ptbo Holdings.

As such the opportunity for the Ptbo Holdings Option to achieve the trust fund's long-term objectives presented is much less than the Trust Fund Option as presented.

9. However, the Trust Fund Option policy formulation would allow Peterborough Holdings to apply for some portion of the funds for its own renewable energy projects. These projects would likely be of lower risk and actually help to stabilize the trust funds income in its early start-up phase.

10. The trust fund 's first recommendation of project plans to review and evaluation and as for-fee project operator, would be to Ptbo Holdings in order to maximize the local investment.

11. It is this separation of the fund source at arm's length from the City of Peterborough and from Ptbo Holdings that has the potential to create more projects more quickly that create more local small and medium investment opportunities that create more local sustainable jobs through the community building the economic multiplier effect and in the end, produce a higher

percentage of local power as a measure of community resilience and as renewables lead to lower local carbon emissions.

D. Expanding the Trust: Embracing the Whole of the City and County's Non-Capital Cost Response to the Climate Crisis Emergency

1. The trust idea has been in the Transition Town Peterborough playbook since its inception in 2007.

    The global transition model addresses the energy, economic and environmental predicament that we are in and deals with all three together at the same time as a system, and in so doing pursues absolute energy descent as well as emissions reduction from the burning of fossil fuels to create a more resilient community to prepare for whatever lies ahead.

    Switching from fossil fuels to renewables is the first mitigation and adaptive step but will not on its own prepare us for the post-carbon economy of 2050 and beyond.

2. Transition Town Peterborough has conducted multiple town halls and follows up group sessions on the formation of a city and county owned investment trust---at the time it was called the "Triple E Trust" representing energy, economics, environment. With the addition of equity as the fourth E, the Transition Town model now talks about the 4 E's Framework.

3. The investment trust idea and focus on building a more resilient community has been left to the non-profit sector and the small amount of money provided by grants and locally owned business sponsors.

    The City and County's efforts were and are about gaining business and NFP support for the Community Sustainability Plan and Climate Change Action Plan with no project plan funding behind them. The result is a public perception of these plans as award programs with little accountability to the Citizens of the City and County of Peterborough.

4. Hopefully, the City Council will take this trust fund recommendation for the management and use of the funds from the sale of PDI as a significant opportunity in its own right and begin the process of expanding the trust to embrace the whole of the City and County's response to the climate crisis emergency.

5. As a brief outline, a **4 E's Operating Investment Trust** would:

   a) Require annual funding from both the City and County of Peterborough (estimated at 1% of respective 2020 operating budgets rising to 2% by 2030)

   b) Clearly define its Community-Based 4 E Resiliency Goals and Objectives

   c) Be composed of at least three entities at this writing including the:

   Renewable Energy Fund created with funds from the sale of PDI

   Climate Crisis Emergency Fund already started by the City of Peterborough and where the bulk of the annual funding from the City and County would go.

   Kawartha Loon Exchange transferring the Currency Issuer from Transition Town to the 4 E's operating investment trust allowing the trust to accept the interest on the Canadian dollar reserve which backs the Kawartha Loon.

   d) Clearly identify the beneficiaries of the trust as the Citizens of the City and County of Peterborough.

5. Expanding the trust to a City and County jointly owned and supported investment trust is the best way to work together and make our community whole in terms of building resilience in life essentials. This is not to say that the negotiating process and trade-offs will easily be digested by either party, but to even think that the City and County can address what lies ahead on their own is beyond comprehension.

6. Lastly, now is the time to face the reality that nothing much that we are doing collectively is enough for our community to fully recover from the social and economic Impact of COVID-19, let alone prepare us for the climate crisis emergency that lies ahead. It, therefore, seems to be the time to think and act boldly in the best interest of the Citizens of the City and County of Peterborough.

E. Appendix A
The Resiliency Imperative & Framework: Building a More Resilient Peterborough by 2030

"Climate change is creating a vicious cycle in which that change creates greater extremes in weather which create more demand for energy which is still largely generated using fossil fuels -which then release more greenhouse gases creating more extreme climate"(Kurt Cobb, Resource Insights).

The only downturn in planetary warming caused by GHG emissions was during the 2008/2009 Great Recession as global economic growth stalled. Despite our collective global efforts, GHG emissions have continued to rise ever since. They are on track to exceed what scientists have identified as the 2030 tipping point of no return from the worst effects of the climate change crisis.

The question before us now is how do we bring the City and County Councils, locally owned businesses and farming enterprises supplying food to the local market, not-for-profit organizations, citizen-led groups and citizens at large to work together on an integrated framework to become more resilient by 2030. This is the resiliency imperative and likely the dominant struggle we face moving forward to 2030.

"Resilience is the capacity of a system to encounter disruption and still maintain its base structure and function" (Richard Heinberg, Fellow, Post Carbon Institute).

The resiliency imperative suggest a balanced framework integrating everyone's work within the 4 E's of the energy, economy, environment, and equity, both social and economic.

From years of study by the transition movement here in Peterborough and around the world, by the New Economy Coalition and the Post Carbon Institute, some things relating to the 4 E's have become very clear.

First: Shifting to renewable sources of energy is highly desirable. However, such a shift will not be sufficient to maintain the complex lifestyles that we currently enjoy. Energy security and community resilience require the need for a significant per capita decrease in the usage of all forms of energy. This is called energy descent and is the foundational direction of the Transition Movement here and around the world.

Second: We ignore building our own community-based economic localization infrastructure at our own peril. Large corporations continue to hollow-out our community, because we don't recognize and support the economic models that build local resilience and security, leading to increased vitality, jobs, prosperity and community renewal through new family formation.

Third: Environmental degradation and social and economic inequities will continue to dominate our political outrage and climate change crisis attention until we re-focus to a balanced approach that addresses energy descent and economic localization infrastructure, the lack thereof being the root causes of both.

Fourth: As a community, we can expect to get financial support from the federal and provincial governments, for some services, shifting energy to renewable sources and for capital projects that support physical infrastructure including low-income housing. However, as the climate change crisis deepens, we can expect that the bulk of the job of building a more resilient and secure community will be up to us!

We can easily relate to the lack of economic localization infrastructure when we start to consider securing our food supply. There is little debate about the probable disruption of our industrial agriculture food supply within the ten years to 2030. The California fire cycle has moved from seasonal to full year and water in many countries and US states supplying us with food is getting much scarcer. Not only will food prices rise for everyone but the working poor and less fortunate are in danger of becoming even less food secure than they already are in the GPA, reportedly one of Canada's most food-insecure regions.

Economic localization infrastructure required to help secure our local food supply includes a local food hub with a year-round farmers' market, storage, and interest-free commercial bank loans supported by the Municipality for local farmers selling into the local market, as well as for other businesses in the local food supply chain. These few ideas are neither new nor exhaustive in terms of gaining much greater food security through building our economic localization infrastructure.

We invite our City and County Councils, every organization, business and citizen in the GPA to focus on what their contribution might be towards building a more Resilient Peterborough by 2030.

Fred Irwin Founding Director
Transition Town Peterborough Inc.
Canada's First Transition Town

F. Appendix B
Resiliency Imperative & 4 E's Framework

(Centrefold as published in *Greenzine* magazine, volume 12, "ResilientPtbo 2030" Edition 2020 available online at www.transitiontownpeterborough.ca)

FOLLOW-UP EMAIL LETTER TO THE PDI INVESTMENT OPTIONS WORKING GROUP WITH RESPECT TO THE VIRTUAL MEETING AND PRESENTATION ON FRIDAY, AUGUST 7, 2020

To the PDI Investment Options Working Group

Re Transition Town Renewable Power Generation Trust Model

Thank you for giving us the opportunity to respond to your questions on our proposal presented on Friday, August 7th.

To paraphrase the sub-committee's last question: What does TTP want the Working Group to take away from our Trust model proposal and follow-up interview?

We clarify and expand on our response with this letter.

With the funds from the sale of PDI, City Council has a unique opportunity to make an impactful and visionary long-term difference to the future resilience of the local Peterborough community and economy.

The goals of our presentation in consideration of the age of resilience that we are entering supported by a near-zero cost energy regime are to:

- offer City Council an innovative method of investing as much of the $50 million-plus as fiscally possible into a local renewable energy model to increase the resilience of the local community well into the future.

- while providing a structural means, with multiple renewable power generation companies and co-operatives, to help build badly needed local economic investment infrastructure for large medium and small local investors to invest in their own community.

The Benefits of this Model:

- The trust model kick-starts local new renewable energy projects with multiple power generation companies and co-operatives.

- The power generation companies leverage more renewable energy investment in our community.

- The visionary trust creates the opportunity for retailing electricity directly from the power source at critical sites around the City strengthening our community resilience.

- At the municipal level, keeping the money invested locally is fiscally responsible management.

- Also, from a municipal perspective, the ROI of the investment cannot be limited to economic ROI.

It is the civic responsibility of Council to consider social equity, the environment, and energy security in their decision-making process. Transition Town Peterborough believes this proposal aids in fulfilling these responsibilities.

It is widely understood and accepted on a global scale that we are moving into what is being called the Third Industrial Revolution. Creating a global marginal cost economy as a measured response to climate change and current real-time global economic and energy disruptors is both prudent and responsible.

Local renewable energy sources are critical to creating local marginal costs and supporting rapidly advancing innovations in robotics and automation. By dealing with potential disruptors proactively, Peterborough as a community would be able to achieve economic, environmental, social and energy stability plus experience continued growth and advancement during certain upcoming challenges.

We provide this video link to Jeremy Rifkin on TVO's "The Agenda," speaking to the Third Industrial Revolution---the Age of Resilience. (embedded link)

Our proposal uses existing Peterborough assets and infrastructure, updates and revolutionizes their potential, and fully supports our energy requirements for future generations.

We look forward to hearing the sub-committee's recommendations and welcome further questions. Transition Town Peterborough is available to offer as much assistance to this process as you feel we can provide. We are 100% transparent and in the public domain.

Transition Town Peterborough Inc.
Fred Irwin, Founding Director
CC TTP Board of Directors

NB Both the PowerPoint Presentation and Jeremy Rifkin's video as linked in the original letter are available on the Transition Town Peterborough website at www.transitiontownpeterborough.ca.

TRENT COMMUNITY RESEARCH CENTRE (TCRC) PROJECT # 4874
Municipal Trust for Operational Funding.

Purpose of the Project as Assigned:

The Purpose is to lever local community financing to serve citizens of Peterborough City and County, locally owned businesses, local charities and not-for-profit organizations in responding to the interconnected energy, economic, environmental and equity impacts of the climate/energy crisis.

The City and County of Peterborough have not yet faced the enormous costs of adapting to the worst effects of the climate crisis, nor do they have the non-political infrastructure to equitably distribute funds to build the local economy. Formation of a public trust could provide a good part of the necessary economic infrastructure to build a more resilient local economy.

Historical Context:

The Transition Towns movement started with an energy descent action plan produced by students as an assignment from a Rob Hopkins class.

Transition Town Peterborough has followed in the footsteps of engaging students wherever possible. TTP utilizes local Trent University first-year students in the operation of our two annual festivals and some are invited to serve on the festivals operating committee.

The Transition Skills Forum has held over 100 workshops at a Trent University student facility and many Trent U students have attended these workshops on a pay-what-you-can basis. In the early formation of TTP, two Trent University students served on the TTP Board of Directors.

A Trent University student completed a TTP/TCRC Research Project in April 2020, titled "Connecting Local Food and Food Security in Peterborough."

TCRC Project # 4874 is underway in December 2020. The project outline is posted on the Trent University TCRC website.

CHAPTER 4 ███████████████
STRATEGIC ROADMAP

For A More Resilient Community by 2030

EXECUTIVE SUMMARY:

June 2020 – This document puts forward the idea that embracing the goal of making the Peterborough Community the most Resilient Community in Canada by 2030 offers the best way forward to deal with the climate crisis emergency as declared by the City of Peterborough.

Further, the document suggests that the pursuit of this goal can provide the best opportunity to frame and develop plans and programs for the COVID-19 recovery, the local jobs crisis, food insecurity crisis and other social and economic injustice issues.

Resiliency is defined as the capacity of a community such as Peterborough to encounter disruption and still maintain its base structure. The disruption could be caused by a climate crisis event or any other crisis such as COVID-19.

All governments have elaborate operating systems and frameworks to provide good governance. Big global businesses that shape and run our consumer economy most everywhere on earth have sophisticated operating systems and frameworks to maximize their own financial return on investment (ROI).

Neither local municipal governments, global corporations, nor local economic development organizations, charities and other not-for-profits working on social justice have an operating system and framework to help guide the community to achieve the goal of becoming the most Resilient Community in Canada by 2030--- the IPCC (Intergovernmental Panel on Climate Change) identified climate crisis tipping point.

The international Transition Towns movement operating system interpreted herein by TTP is offered as the best system to be adopted by the City and County of Peterborough to lead our community towards the goal of the most Resilient Community in Canada by 2030.

The Transition Towns operating system explained in more detail herein is permaculture about the design of permanent agriculture systems and of equal importance the design of more permanent cultural systems---the way we live. The permaculture operating system is supported by the balance of the 4 E's Framework (energy, economy, environment, and equity, both social and economic) with a focus on the security of life essentials, including food, water, energy, culture and wellness.

The first E is energy. It is at a critical juncture in Peterborough with the sale of PDI to Hydro One generating cash to the City of Peterborough and the Citizens of Peterborough of from $50 million to $55 million---likely by August this year.

With the Resilient Community Goal to 2030 set in place with the permaculture operating system, it is suggested that as much of the $50 million to $55 million as possible be reinvested into the community energy sector from whence it came, along with any return on that investment so that the community can advance to become more energy secure and resilient while also offering more local investment opportunities and more local sustainable jobs.

The permaculture design operating system and the goal of greater local energy security led to the TTP proposal of the Renewable

Power Generation Investment Trust Fund as submitted to the City of Peterborough and shown herein in Section M, Appendix A.

As suggested in Appendix A, the Investment Trust could be logically expanded to include non-capital funding, in support of the climate crisis emergency. Consistent with the direction of this Strategic Roadmap a more appropriate name for the fund would be the Community Resiliency Fund (CRF) either inside or outside the Trust with annual contributions from both the City and County of up to 2% of their respective operating budgets by 2030.

Projects that would be eligible for immediate funding from the Community Resiliency Fund as outlined in this Strategic Roadmap are as follows:

1. Home energy retrofit program offering to pay the interest on qualified commercial bank loans of up to $50,000 for up to 10 years.

2. Local-food-farmer loans to pay the interest on qualified commercial bank loans of up to $50,000 for up to 10 years. Qualified applications would include greenhouses, storage facilities and other farm equipment.

3. Funding for a Trent Community Research Centre (TCRC) project to complete a 50% local food economic impact analysis and jobs report for 50% Local Food 2030 in the Peterborough Community.

4. Local-food supply-chain loans to pay the interest on qualified commercial bank loans of up to $50,000 for up to 10 years.

5. Pilot funding to TTP for the Transition Neighbourhoods Project specifically designed as an energy descent initiative.

6. Funding to TTP for scaling to community size its two long-standing community resiliency building festivals in the

downtown core area. These are the Peter Patch LocalPalooza and the Purple Onion Harvest Festival.

7. Funding to TTP and/or a City and County Trust or PKED to convert the Kawartha Loon local currency to an electronic currency supported by the print version as a boost to economic localization infrastructure and a quantum leap in the local economic multiplier effect created by locally owned businesses' increased trading with each other as well as with their own customers.

8. Funding to TTP to develop the I Love Local Food Peterborough Downtown Culinary Hub Brand.

9. Funding to Green Up and TTP and others to provide team leadership and mentor volunteer support to neighbourhood groups to implement sponge streets.

Local food is highlighted as the complete food for advancing towards a more resilient community with more vitality and the lowering of our carbon footprint. Local food impacts all 4 E's in the permaculture system framework. It is the complete food to adapt to the climate change crisis, help the economic recovery from the COVID-19 pandemic, respond to the local jobs crisis and make the community less food insecure, helping to solve some of the social and economic inequity issues that exist in our community. *equity working c Kawartha food Share, One rook, Salvator*

Leadership in local food starts with the City and County coming together and setting the goal of achieving 50% local food of home and restaurant consumption measured in dollars by 2030.

With the local food goal in place, municipal leadership representing the City and County is recommended to be provided by the Peterborough and Kawarthas Economic Development Corporation (PKED).

PKED is recommended to lead a community task force to evaluate and provide the concept design of a physical local food hub.

It is recommended that the City of Peterborough purchase at least two local farms to be sold over time to worker/farmer co-ops to help develop more young farmers in the area.

It is suggested that the City Council signal that the downtown core is considered the economic and cultural centre of the City worthy of significant investment and development.

The process to put that strategy in motion would be confirmed by choosing a downtown site for the replacement Memorial Centre and the assurance of a building design that takes energy conservation and even sourcing its own energy as a top priority.

Further, the Memorial Centre replacement building downtown should immediately signal significant changes to the transportation system and streetscape through the downtown core.

Further, the Memorial Centre replacement building downtown should immediately trigger the review of the highest and best use of building stock in Downtown Peterborough to heighten the cultural vitality of the downtown core.

All of the capital cost projects in the downtown core area, including transportation, likely cannot be fully implemented by 2030. The key is to get started on an integrated plan that the private sector understands so it can enhance investments along the same time frame.

Section K summarizes the importance of social and economic equity as we pursue the goal of becoming the most resilient community in Canada by 2030.

Section L provides 10 key actions on the resiliency timeline.

A. INTRODUCTION:

The intent of this document is to provide a Roadmap to build towards a more vibrant resilient and prosperous Peterborough Community by 2030:

- A community that supports new family formation.

- Supports social and economic equity and justice.

- Qualifies as one of Canada's most resilient communities.

- Ranks among the highest in community well-being.

The reference to the Peterborough Community includes all of the Citizens of the City of Peterborough and the adjoining townships and First Nations within Peterborough County including the Villages of Millbrook and Lakefield.

The 2030 reference point comes from the Intergovernmental Panel on Climate Change (IPCC). Its latest report identifies 2030 as the tipping point of no return from the worst effects of the climate crisis. By now thousands of scientists worldwide have concluded that the CO_2 PPM equivalent in the global atmosphere already exceeds the 2030 tipping point leading to the need for a strategic change from mitigation to adaptation and worldwide resilience building at the community level.

Annual CO_2 emissions keep rising, and only declined during the Great Recession in 2008/2009. Emissions are expected to drop again during the global economic downturn resulting from the COVID-19 pandemic but even a resulting deep global recession or depression will not change the 2030 tipping point timing... it's already dialed in!

The Transition Towns' global movement and model created by Rob Hopkins in Totnes, UK, in 2005/2006 accepted the then high probability presented by the (IPCC) models that the tipping point for no return was 2030. It then proceeded to help educate and demonstrate to the world how to build resilient communities.

Hundreds of books in many languages now reference and recognize the Transition Towns model for building community resilience.

The first Transition Towns initiative emerged from a 2004 Rob Hopkins university students' project to utilize permaculture as the design system to produce an energy descent action plan. This first action plan became the foundation of the worldwide Transition Towns movement and permaculture became the fundamental design system with a set of principles values and ethics.

The importance of the permaculture design system to the resolution of the predicaments we are now in globally and locally will permeate this document. And it is an objective of this document to have the City and County of Peterborough adopt permaculture as their respective operating systems to lead the community to achieve resiliency goals.

Transition Town Peterborough (TTP) founded in 2007 as Canada's First Transition Town has been formally recognized as such by the City of Peterborough.

TTP has reached thousands of local residents through its festivals, town halls, feedback sessions, film showings, resiliency building and permaculture seminars along with transition training focused on Resilient Peterborough 2030--- most by community experts, free or pay-what-you-can. The TTP *Greenzine* quarterly free print version of 5,000 copies has been delivered locally for 12 years and the online publication not only reaches over 3,000 local households but is seen throughout the Transition Towns World.

TTP is a member of the international Transition Towns network and also a supporter of the New Economy Coalition and the Post Carbon Institute relying on all three sources for expert analysis and opinions to advance local resilience here in the Peterborough Community,

B. NOW IS THE TIME!

Crisis creates an opportunity for bold, accelerated change.

This axiom holds true despite our extremely slow response to the global climate crisis now declared an emergency by the City of Peterborough.

Now we have crisis upon crisis that demands our attention.

There is nowhere else to hide. Our house is on fire!

This document is intended to make the case that recovery from all of these crises is not a problem that can be easily solved. Rather it is a predicament that we must deal with together and not using perfection or purity of mission as a compromise for advancing together with a common goal.

We first set out the goal of making the Peterborough Community the most Resilient Community in Canada by 2030.

We document the crises that we face as a community as follows: climate change, COVID-19 pandemic, systemic racism pandemic, local jobs crisis, local food insecurity crisis, and economic recession, all leading to more local systemic social and economic inequity if positive plans for immediate action are not put in place!

Without an operating system and a systems framework to prioritize and get on with the work together the task seems overwhelming, and the goal seems remote and unimportant.

However, the Transition model, approaching 15 years in age has matured with 13 years in Peterborough, is ready to offer a system design way forward against the goal of building the most Resilient Community in Canada by 2030.

Now is the time for accelerated change!

C. RENEWABLE ENERGY INVESTMENT:

Because the issue of how to invest the funds from the sale of PDI to Hydro One is already before City Council, we start with a dialogue on renewable energy investment and include the TTP Proposal to reinvest these funds in a renewable power generation trust fund intended to firstly increase the amount of renewable power generated locally while leveraging local investment and engagement to create more jobs in the Peterborough Community.

The importance of this decision is reinforced by the reality that it is likely the largest amount of discretionary cash that City Council will deal with for years to come and where and how it is invested will largely signal the future direction of our community.

Energy is the first of the 4 E's in the Transition Towns system framework and also one of the five life essentials that need to be secured to create a resilient community in any time frame. The other four are food, water, culture and wellness.

A brief analysis of the Transition history in Peterborough would reveal that the 4 E's and the five life essentials permeate everything we do. The life essentials were first identified in the reference document, titled "Strategic Framework for the Economic Localization of the City & County of Peterborough." Version 2.0 was completed in 2013 by TTP and was posted on the TTP website for five years.

Emissions Reduction: It is highly desirable to switch our energy sources from fossil fuels to renewables to decrease CO_2 equivalent emissions. In Peterborough, those renewables are likely to be small-scale hydroelectric, solar, wind, biogas, geothermal all of which take enormous amounts of fossil fuels to produce. Many projects have marginal EROEI's and marginal ROI's.

EROEI stands for energy return on energy invested as the key indicator of sustainable projects. However, in a world crying out for sustainable and renewable local energy sources, they all have to be evaluated. The

ROI is the monetary return on investment. Unfortunately, we live in an upside-down world where many projects in the name of emissions reduction have positive ROI's and near-zero or negative EROEI's. These projects are not sustainable and do nothing to build resilience at any level.

Even if we eliminated all fossil fuels the world over by 2030 (i.e., oil, natural gas, coal, and all its derivatives) the predicament of runaway climate change events affecting all life on the planet on ice, land, sea, and freshwater bodies will remain with us.

This simple reality is important when we think of the allocation of Citizens' Funds in the City and County of Peterborough. Do we invest in emissions reduction projects or in building community resilience which by design will also reduce emissions?

The permaculture operating system directs us to always think of the long term to what is the most permanent and the most resilient before we trade-off to the most economic and expedient.

As an example, let's take the electric bus idea--- what a great idea, eh! However, there is no evidence that when all the virtual fossil fuels and rare earths are included from its manufacture that it will have a positive EROEI or positive emissions reduction over its useful life. That is not to say that early adoption of electric buses might not very well stimulate a new positive resiliency direction for the City. *electric Bus*

However, an electric bus unto itself will not make our community more resilient, and right now we might want to invest the equivalent dollar amounts in aggressive energy descent that will guarantee emission reduction, more local jobs and much greater community resilience. And such a program, called the Transition Neighbourhoods Project, already exists and is ready for funding from the City to proceed to the Pilot Phase.

So for now let us sing the praises of EROEI towards the understanding of the huge amount of energy in a barrel of oil that has facilitated the creation of every aspect of our complex society.

Ode to Renewable Energy (to the tune of Old McDonald had a farm)

Old man River had a dream EROEI!
In that dream, he saw some things EROEI!

First the sun then solar too
With lots of wind coming through EROEI!

And on the farm a pile of poo.
With the biogas promise shining through EROEI.

And now we know all that renewables can do.
By securing our energy sources through and through.

E R O E I

Energy as a life essential makes its security the name of the game.

We focus on producing local decentralized renewable energy for energy security which builds resilience in our community. If we do this, we are better positioned to face an uncertain future that is more and more reliant on complex technology that requires more and more energy. The 5G internet is an example. No one knows how much energy is required to run the system and nobody knows who will bear the ultimate cost to make it available to everyone to answer the resiliency need for social equity.

For now, all the renewable power generated by our local power company is fed into the Hydro One grid under the FIT (Feed-In-Tariff) program. All of the residential and privately owned Micro-FIT installations are also fed into the grid. These are all one-way flow into the centralized grid offering little or no energy security for the Peterborough Community... it won't always be thus.

Many of these Micro-FIT contracts will be expiring within the next 15 years. Meanwhile much more electrical energy will be required to drive the new economy through the expanding tech sector. Indeed, the new economy trend is towards a two-way flow of energy between the centralized grid and decentralized power inputs and electric vehicle battery storage. Entropy, representing the second law of thermodynamics, alone makes this a very low-efficiency option at a time when the key global economic metric is moving very rapidly from GDP economic growth to the efficient use of energy in all its forms.

The more electrical energy we can generate locally for our own requirements the more secure we are as a community.

It's not money we are short of as proven during this COVID-19 pandemic but the equitable distribution of energy in all its forms, including food. However, the new higher energy usage economy is coming at us like an out-of-control freight train, eventually dragging along much higher costs because of its lower efficiency. This opens the social-equity issue of who among us can afford to be electronically connected.

The phenomenon is already evident in Canada and around the world only to be exposed most recently within the systemic racism pandemic. Black Lives Matter and a much higher percentage of these lives heralded in Canada by the likes of the Chamber of Commerce as productive diversity cannot afford to be connected. Shall we add Canada's First Nations Peoples to this crisis as well as the scores of New Canadians not yet assimilated into our culture?

And now we have exposed two types of workers instead of the 20th Century rich, middle class and poor. Suddenly we have essential workers who must work no matter what, including the police, firefighter, the FedEx delivery person, the health care worker, the bus driver, the pizza delivery person and on and on while the rest of us remain in our homes working and playing on 5G waiting for the delivery of our dinner and the latest new device offered on Amazon. It's all a recipe to build runaway social injustice in our society as it turns out that a disproportionate number of our essential workers are black and brown, poorer and less healthy than the rest of us.

b/c they need to survive

This complex cultural system built around the internet is subject to cyber- attacks and just ordinary hackers as well as countless breakdowns from climate change events driving communities like Peterborough to invest in stand-alone off-grid power generation systems using grid power as an occasional backup and a place to sell excess power.

The TTP proposal submitted to the City of Peterborough for the investment of funds from the sale of PDI to Hydro One outlined some of the key renewable power generation projects that could be leveraged for development. That report is attached as Appendix A (Now in this book presented in Chapter 3).

Further, the $50 million Trust investment in renewable energy could provide the leverage for Cavan Monaghan to come to the table on the annexation of lands suitable for development for manufacturing businesses to bring more jobs to the community to help increase our local resilience. This is one way to help the local jobs crisis by working together. Negotiations need to be re-opened ASAP to build towards much greater community resilience enhancing both parties.

It further seems almost mandatory to implement serious energy descent action plans that increase local resilience throughout the commercial and residential built community in both the City and County to thrive in an uncertain world of higher energy costs. The previously mentioned Transition Neighbourhoods Project is a proven energy descent initiative based on behavioural economics and peer-to-peer engagement at the neighbourhood level. A TTP Pilot Proposal will be made to the City of Peterborough for startup implementation this year.

This short brief on energy is not intended to diminish the City's and County's work to put in the regulations required for how new neighbourhoods can be formed and built fully integrated with the permaculture operating system advocated herein reducing the amount of energy consumed in all its forms.

Further, if we invest our energy dollars carefully in a number of small- to medium-sized renewable energy projects, not only can we increase our overall energy security as a community, but we can create a number of economic infrastructure projects that can attract local small- and medium-sized investors as well as loans from commercial banks all investing in our community.

Such projects would include the regional hospital, the new Memorial Centre replacement, the repurposed existing Memorial Centre, Trent University, local food hub, Fleming College, downtown heritage buildings, and any electrified public transportation system to name some of the most critical projects.

With respect to investing PDI sale funds into a residential or commercial energy retrofit program, the permaculture operating system suggests that this would be an unnecessary transfer of the $50 million public capital base to the private sector without a lot of leverage.

Although a residential retrofit program is necessary, such a program would ideally combine provincial and federal grants, commercial bank and mortgage loans together with the interest on the net project cost being covered by the expanded trust fund account as supported by annual contributions from the City and County of Peterborough. This expanded trust fund account is covered in the "Renewable Power Generation Investment Trust Fund Proposal" formally submitted to the City of Peterborough as shown in Appendix A Attached (Shown in this book in Chapter 3).

D. RESILIENCY IMPERATIVE
CHANGING LIFESTYLES:

The COVID-19 pandemic has resulted in the largest lifestyle changes in Peterborough, in Canada and around the world since the Second World War. It reminds us all of what we can do together if our lives depend on it as individuals and as a Peterborough Community.

The COVID-19 pandemic still exists and hasn't been beaten with either therapies or a vaccine but we came together with unified leadership and with a health care system, although much less than perfect, one that did not get in the way of advancing radical action in quick order to move us all to a more resilient place from which we can eradicate the virus.

The same type of process that we are experiencing with the eradication of the COVID-19 pandemic is advocated for the recovery plan from COVID-19 and it is indeed inherent in the permaculture operating system at the foundation of the Transition Towns model for building resilient communities.

> *"Resilience is the capacity of a system to encounter disruption and still maintain its base structure and function"* (Richard Heinberg, Post Carbon Institute).

The system we are talking about is the way the Peterborough Community functions.

The disruptions we are encountering in real-time are the crises already identified including climate change, COVID-19 pandemic, local jobs and growing social, racial and economic inequities.

The Resiliency Imperative before us now is how do we bring City and County Councils, locally owned businesses and farming enterprises supplying food to our local market, not-for-profit organizations, charities, business associations, citizen-led groups and citizens at large to work together within the same operating system with one operational framework to work on all of the crises at hand in integration at the same time to become a more Resilient Community by 2030.

Both the City and County of Peterborough have well-organized systems of governance in place with an active framework of individual departments responsible for issues that are budgeted and elevated to their respective councils in a department-specific manner. The system lacks flexibility and a sense of urgency in the face of crisis.

Neither the City nor County have a long-term goal nor operating system that addresses societal change to achieve that goal or a framework to turn plans into actions. Official plans as operating systems created at the municipal level are most often overcome by the accelerating speed of change and therefore are often dead on arrival or simply ignored by incoming Councils.

Large global corporations drive our consumer society and our local governance. They have the money, power and influence to create change. They have very clear goals, sophisticated, flexible, automated feedback systems in place to achieve their goals and integrated frameworks to get the job done. The multiple crises we are now faced with are often collateral damage or externalities to the winners in the global competition for the monetization of every human need (real or perceived) creating continuous economic growth as the only worthy metric for the way we live.

The only way forward to make some sense of the multiple crises and to deal with them head-on seems to be to begin the active implementation of the localization strategy as pursued by Transition Towns here in Peterborough and around the world.

Before that discussion, let's talk about the operating system that keeps us on track as we pursue our goal.

E. PERMACULTURE OPERATING SYSTEM:

Our goal is to become the most Resilient Community in Canada by 2030.

We already have multiple crises that are disrupting our ability to achieve that goal, and we don't want to be knocked off our timeline to achieve that goal.

So now is the time to adopt permaculture as our operating system to move forward as a community.

A brief detour on the origin of permaculture takes us to Tasmania, Australia, in the 1970s when Bill Mollinson and David Holmgen devised the principles of permaculture which are part of the DNA of every certified official Transition Towns initiative in the world. In the case of TTP, the permaculture principles are written into our Charter and have become the signature operating system for everything we do and propose.

Permaculture is a system of agriculture and social design principles around the way we grow our food and live, utilizing the patterns and features observed in natural systems.

The permaculture principles are the most significant in the human design for security of life essentials, including the air we breathe, the food, water and energy we consume supporting our wellness and culture.

> "The aim of permaculture is to create ecologically sound, economically prosperous human communities. It is guided by a set of ethical principles – care for the earth, care for people, and sharing the surplus" (Gaia's Garden: A Guide to Home-Scale Permaculture, Toby Hemenway, 2000).

So how does permaculture work as a design system in a non-agricultural situation? As the permaculture word implies, the principles guide us to look for the most permanent solution which in natural systems means the most flexible or adaptive or, in permaculture speak, resilient solution.

As applies to recovery from COVID-19, let's talk about the restaurants downtown. The City COO now has the authority to allow more outdoor space for restaurants for the summer tourist season. That indeed seems like a good thing on the surface but will likely be plagued by division and unanticipated issues.

Why? Because there is no consensus operating system that would make it clear to all the system constituents, including building owners, restaurant operators, local residents, potential tourists that we as a community are striving to become the most Resilient City in Canada by 2030.

If that simple goal were to be put in place, the downtown would quickly be understood and declared as the economic engine for the whole community and every effort and program would be designed to make it so. Building owners and restaurant operators would be incentivized to begin to invest capital against a long-term plan.

The number one tourist draw to Peterborough would become the downtown core sitting on the sparkling Little Lake. Instead, and despite the gallant efforts of DBIA (Downtown Business Improvement Association), it is being left to decline because of lack of investment, yes--- but also the lack of understanding of how to build resilient communities. This document will expand on this throughout on how to make the downtown part of the solution to all the crises we face towards building a more resilient community.

One more point is that if we understood the downtown as the community's strategic economic driver, our heart and soul, we wouldn't dream of hiring an outside consultant to tell us where we should build a Memorial Centre replacement. But rather we would simply ask a local engineering firm to advise where in the downtown core it should be placed. We realize that there may well be a municipal governance system for such a simple ask to be made without a request for proposal. However, that only serves to reinforce how far the city governance design system has moved away from replicating natural systems such as the system of permaculture design offers. How about the police solution

Another example, again with respect to the investment of the $50 million from the sale of PDI: If you look at our local energy generation and supply as one system--- as a community we are taking $50 million of our citizen-generated capital out of the system. In a review of all proposals made for the investment of the $50 million capital, all of them recognized that the permaculture yield, called return on investment or interest, needed to be invested back into the community.

However, only two of the proposals, namely the Ptbo Holdings Option and the Transition Trust Fund, recognized that all the capital as well needs to be reinvested back into the community renewable energy system in conformance with permaculture system design principles for community resilience.

To suggest otherwise is to perpetuate the capital drain from the Peterborough Community that has been going on too long. We understand that Hydro One is reinvesting a $105 million that yields the $50 million net. However, how to invest the $50 million capital should come down to where in the new community renewable energy system can we get the most leverage and long-term return from the investment.

The permaculture systems objectives were set out in the Transition Town Trust Fund Proposal which integrates the permaculture systems framework and sets out objectives in Section B Trust Fund Leading Objectives. Reference Appendix A Attached (Shown in this book as Chapter 3).

F. 4 E'S FRAMEWORK:

What do we need a Framework for?

The Transition Towns movement started out identifying the Environmental global Crisis as an interconnected predicament of issues involving peak oil, climate change and Global Capitalism's need for continuous economic growth to support the system of money creation as debt. This interconnected predicament was accompanied by the deep understanding of the huge amount of energy in fossil fuels that provided most of the energy that created our very complex global culture---mostly oil. By around 2005 we had reached the global peak production of conventional oil at around 75 million barrels a day.

By 2008/2009 and the advent of the Great Recession, the price of a barrel of oil peaked at $147 US per barrel. All oil is monetized in US dollars. The Great Recession has been blamed on the bursting of the subprime

are we headed that way

mortgage bubble in the USA as owners with mortgages underwater (higher than the value of their homes) had to choose between the lesser of two evils---staying in their homes or affording gas in their cars to go to work to put food on the table for their families.

The Great Recession became global either because of the global spike in the price of oil or the fact that the US subprime mortgage market had fled to investment by financial institutions around the globe.

Either way, the recession was real and scary and global.

Within the Transition Towns movement, peak oil broadened to global energy and its interaction with global economics. The two became entrenched and both became part of the global degradation of our global environment.

The well-established permaculture system driving the Transition Towns movement almost required that effective solutions had to deal with all three E's (energy, economics, environment) at the same time to create any real progress towards the goal of building community resilience.

After intellectually struggling with the understanding that if you wanted to build true community resilience, you could not leave anyone behind, even though the Transition Towns model was always inclusive with free or pay-what-you-can events, the fourth E for Equity both social and economic was added to our framework for the design of resilient communities.

Equity

The Triple E Framework became the 4 E's Framework

The art of the 4 E's Framework is to be able to think systemically across each E with a permaculture-systems approach in the prioritization and ultimate resolution of all issues within the multiple crises we face. While doing this together the focus is on maximizing the effectiveness of each solution across the framework and not sub-optimizing the goal of becoming the most Resilient Community in Canada.

In the process of making this happen over and over again with skilled leadership, the end goal begins to look more and more achievable.

For one, you might very well ask how the Transition Neighbourhoods Project addresses the 4 E's and builds community resilience. We will answer that in a project proposal to the City of Peterborough.

G. LEADERSHIP:

The first job of leadership in any crisis is to get everyone together in some sort of partnership or alliance working on solutions together with full transparency.

The second job is to clearly enunciate a common goal and repeatedly communicate and explain why and how we expect to achieve that goal as we work together.

In a crisis or in a situation where we have multiple crises at the same time as we do right now, progress has to be communicated regularly on schedule, daily, weekly or monthly or whatever is appropriate on each and every issue being dealt with.

The next job for leadership is to put in place the structure for the equitable distribution of funding to support actions. That is, where is the money coming from and how do constituents access it?

Then as the Japanese say and do nemawashi. ← What's that?

The leadership communication of the COVID-19 pandemic offers outstanding examples of leadership communications at our national, provincial and local level---simply no magic here---leader's failure to communicate with full transparency becomes a detriment to their own success and their constituents pay the price. In 2020 it's difficult to lead from a bunker. Citizens are connected in real-time like no other time in our history.

lacking in Mayor -) communication

In the Peterborough Community, the leadership title belongs to the mayor of the City supported by the City Council all in partnership with the County warden and County Council and adjoining township mayors and Councils and First Nation chiefs and Councils--- these individuals make up our collective governmental leadership.

This collective governmental leadership has to realize that the municipal governance systems they are comfortable with are ill-prepared to make good decisions in accelerated time frames to work through the crisis predicaments that we are in as a people in the Peterborough Community.

At least on the COVID-19 recovery issue, our prime minister has recognized this at the national level and our provincial premier at the provincial level and our City mayor appear not to be far behind in partnership with the County warden.

However, none of the three levels of government have yet to fully understand the permaculture system and 4 E's Systems Framework offered in this document. The federal government has however signaled their support for building Resilient Communities, recognizing the reality that it is up to citizens at the local level to build a better future for their own well-being.

It's up to us! Let's get after it!

H. LOCALIZATION STRATEGY:

Praise for *The Local Economy Solution: Reinventing economic development as if small business mattered* by Michael H Shuman, 2015.

"Micheal Shuman is the world's most knowledgeable cheerleader and observer of efforts to promote local economies... If you have any interest in furthering your region's economic resilience, this brilliant, clear book should be at the very top of your reading list" (Richard Heinberg, Post Carbon Institute).

Building community has always required a robust localization strategy. It is not an isolation strategy in any way--- no doubt an impossible task in the time of the 5G internet.

To build a resilient community we start by focusing on life essentials.

Transition Town Peterborough outlined life essentials early in its existence as food, water, energy culture, and wellness. Everything TTP does is focused on these. Practically, we need to include air for sure and the transition movement certainly does in terms of its focus on limiting emissions to reduce our environmental impact.

On Energy:

Housing is often suggested as a critical life essential, and it is. However, it is considered part of energy or more specifically the way we harvest and use our energy. In our complex society, some argue that transportation and access to the internet are life essentials. Again, in the transition life essentials model transportation and the internet are part of energy.

While talking about energy as a life essential, let's talk about oil, a bit more as the major fossil fuel that has driven the creation of our now global complex society. Just before COVID-19 struck, the world was consuming 100 million barrels of oil a day. Earlier in Section F, we mentioned that oil production peaked at 75 million barrels a day and $147 US per barrel causing or increasing the severity of the 2008/2009 Great Recession---take your pick.

During the Great Recession we were talking about only conventional oil--- the black stuff we see in films shooting high into the sky from a drilled well. This stuff, when first discovered, had an EROEI as high as 100 to 1 and a cost at the wellhead in Saudi Arabia as low as $1 US per barrel. Now, conventional oil in Saudi Arabia and around the world has EROEI 's more like 30 to 1 at a much higher cost per barrel as prime wells are depleted.

Now we have deep sea oil, Arctic oil, tight or shale oil from fracking, and Canadian tar sands oil collectively known as unconventional oil making up the difference between declining volumes and quality of conventional oil and the total daily global consumption requirement. Here is the rub... unconventional oil EROEI's are much lower than even the declining sources of conventional oil and the costs are much higher at the wellhead.

To get our head around the importance of energy in our way of life and the need to secure it locally, we need to appreciate that our global complex society is driven by the excess amount of energy we have, rather than by the actual amount that is delivered from a well, solar panel, wind generator, nuclear power plant and more. Until we get to nuclear fusion, nuclear power plants can't be considered sources of renewable energy the way they are often portrayed in Ontario.

EROEI's for all known renewable sources of energy are much less than we get from a barrel of oil.

Fracked oil and tar sands oil employ amazing technologies, however, both have very marginal EROEI's and actually negative in some cases.

The bottom line is that a switch to renewable energy sources will not allow most of the inhabitants on the planet to live in the complex society we have designed unless we reduce the net per capita use of all forms of energy---this is the definition of energy descent and the fundamental focus of the Transition Towns movement.

The previously mentioned Transition Neighbourhoods Project is an energy descent project.

The other critical point about energy is that as a Peterborough Community we need to secure as much of our energy as possible for our local consumption. This essentially amounts to developing local renewable sources of energy replacing fossil fuels--- gasoline, natural gas and coal.

Appendix A Attached is TTP's Proposal to the City of Peterborough, titled "Renewable Power Generation Investment Trust Fund," which spells out the leading objectives of such a Trust designed to achieve much greater energy security (Shown in this book as Chapter 3).

On Food:

It's fairly obvious that food is a life essential. What about local food? It is quickly becoming a life essential as well. Using the 4 E's framework, not only is local food more nutritious, but on **E** for Energy, Local food is an energy descent program. On **E** for Economics, local food is likely the number one job creator and economic localization stimulator in our community. On **E** for Environment, local food reduces carbon emissions, and on **E** for Equity, both social and economic, arguably local food offers the best opportunity to advance in both areas---even greater than affordable housing.

Remembering the Great Recession of 2008/2009, people in the US left their homes to put gas in their cars to go to work to buy food to feed their families. If the real estate bubble bursts again as a result of the COVID-19 Recession, we could move to a US depression that goes global at warp speed because of the interconnected global financial markets.

So, local food is the complete food for advancing towards a more resilient community with more vitality and a lower carbon footprint. It is the complete food to fight climate change to recover from COVID-19, to respond to the jobs crisis, to make the community less food insecure, solving some of our social and economic inequity issues.

With farm country all around why have we not embraced local food and indeed rather become one of the most food-insecure cities in Canada? It is the most outrageous problem we have in our community and the easiest for us to come together and begin to fix---If we don't, we will watch the lineups to our food banks grow and grow.

And yet, the City and County of Peterborough seem to have little attention or money to do anything about it and actually continue to make local food less viable in our community.

Transition Town Peterborough is engaged in many initiatives around local food, including Local Food Month, the Purple Onion Harvest Festival, the I Love Local Food Peterborough Brand, the Downtown Local Food Culinary Hub and the 50% Local Food 2030 Project and again as part of the Transition Neighbourhoods Project. All of the TTP projects are underfunded and there is no functioning entity to relate to within the City or County.

This Strategic Roadmap will be making the case for substantial capital and operational funding for local food.

It would be a huge mistake to not leverage the power of volunteerism and active organizations engaged in local food development, such as the Farmers' Markets, Nourish, Community Gardens, Future of Food and Farming SPP Task Force, other organizations and TTP.

Long-term co-ordination and leadership and some funding should exist within the Peterborough and the Kawarthas Economic Development Corporation as it embraces both the City and County. Such responsibility has existed in PKED in the past only to become much less than effective because of the opposing forces between cash-crop farming and farming selling food into the local market.

These forces have to be balanced with strong leadership and the intelligent use of the power of the purse between the City and County and the Province.

No such leadership currently exists. As a result, we have witnessed the fragmentation of farmers' markets in the City with nowhere for all citizens to come together regularly around local food and in the process build local food security.

local food in the public sphere.

It is recommended that the City immediately adopt the goal of achieving 50% local food as applied to home and local restaurant consumption by 2030. This compares to the original Sustainable Peterborough Plan goal approved by the City and County to feed ourselves by the mid-2030s.

It is noted here that the non-capital cost projects could be funded from the Trust as recommended in the investment trust fund recommendation made by TTP supported by annual cash infusions each year from both the City and County. See Appendix A (Shown in this book as Chapter 3).

Action items in support of achieving the goal of 50% Local Food 2030

Fund the TTP proposal designed for TCRC Trent University master's students to complete an economic impact and jobs analysis of 50% local food by 2030. This can be monitored in partnership with PKED if they are funded to support local food. The intent of the economic impact analysis is to provide the rationale for more significant investment in local food as a key driver for greater food security and community resilience.

Transition Town Peterborough postponed its 10th Annual Purple Onion Harvest Festival until the fall of 2021 because of COVID-19. A request for funding will be made to the City of Peterborough or the Trust Fund to scale this festival to community size and create a stronger presence for the Local Food Downtown Culinary Hub.

Assuming PKED takes on the City and County responsibility for local food it is recommended that they create a task force to investigate the services, location and economic return on investment of a physical regional food hub supporting only local food.

The Transition Town 50% Local Food 2030 Project model for such a hub has included an indoor/ outdoor farmers' market run by a farmers' co-op, washing preparation and storage facilities, committee meeting room, local food year-round restaurant, as well as its own on-site energy source. If located at Morrow Park the renewable power source could be a small-scale biogas plant fed by the hub and local area restaurant green waste.

The 50% Local Food 2030 Transition Town model suggests the City purchase at least two local farms of between 50 and 100 acres each to be sold over time to farm worker co-ops in order to develop a younger pool of farmers in the community. These would be capital purchases and budgeted for in the 2021 City plan.

The City of Peterborough or the expanded Investment Trust needs to begin a program to pay the interest on commercial bank loans of up to $50 thousand for 10 years for farm buildings, equipment, greenhouses, washing facilities and storage, and to offer the same loan amount to other businesses in the local food supply chain.

On Water:

If the City ever attempted to privatize its water supply, community outrage would be unprecedented.

Strangely, there are countries in the world where this is happening rather routinely. *-) Philliphians*

We are grateful that the City provides its citizens with a safe water supply.

It would help the community to understand energy much better if we understood the cost and amount of energy required to purify our potable water, pump and distribute the water, and finally, deal with the waste water and storm water streams.

The confusion about energy and water was amplified this spring when in the interest of energy conservation and cost considerations and the climate crisis emergency, City Council tied itself in knots with antiquated governance over a proposal to reduce the run time of the Little Lake Water Fountain.

Certainly, if we had the goal to become the most Resilient Community in Canada by 2030 in place with the permaculture operating system in support, the water fountain debate would at least have some relevant context.

With regard to storm water---the city seems to be rebuilding its commercial streets storm water systems. There is no real way for a citizen at large to evaluate progress or the lack thereof until the next severe storm or river flood hits.

However, with respect to low traffic residential neighbourhood streets, the idea of reducing street and driveway pavement and expanding boulevards should be implemented quickly with neighbourhood citizens group creating what has come to be known as sponge cities. Green Up is already engaged in this practice along with DBIA in the downtown area. The process could be added to the Transition Neighbourhoods Project from an educational perspective. There should be small amounts of money available from the City to be matched by neighbourhood groups and homeowners to get the job done much more quickly while beautifying their own neighbourhoods and increasing their own property values.

With respect to the control and consumption of bottled water, we recommend that the lead should remain with our local Council of Canadians Chapter that has often partnered with TTP.

On Wellness:

Securing our wellness as a community is an important life essential. The idea of community wellness is completely aligned with the goal of building a more resilient community. In fact, the locally owned business owners in the wellness market sector along with local farmers are the constituents that instinctively understand the transition permaculture operating system and building community resilience as a goal.

Within the transition movement, we have identified the wellness sector as the second-largest new jobs opportunity in Peterborough after local food. Many are regular users of the Kawartha Loon local currency. The use of the KL local currency has been most successful in these two sectors only to be disrupted by the declining use of print currency globally and now the COVID-19 pandemic.

The KL local currency was conceived to offset some of the inequities that exist in our current economic system in addition to increasing the economic multiplier effect. The concept of taking the KL electronic is presented later in this Strategic Roadmap.

With respect to wellness, our upside-down energy /economic system leads to two very clear economic inequities that no level of government has so far taken on: healthy local food costs more than industrially farmed highly processed imported food that is less healthy, and local wellness providers who could reduce the total cost of health care are not covered by our universal health care system.

The transition movement encourages personal resilience as a necessary first step towards building a resilient community. Resilient communities are built on the backs of resilient leaders and resilient people who are willing to share their time, energy, and ideas and life experiences with others to build our community. This is a fundamental value of the permaculture operating system practiced in the transition movement around the world.

The Transition Towns experience, since its inception in 2007, has demonstrated a Peterborough Community of willing, competent volunteers to share a whole range of wellness modalities in small group settings at the Transition Skills Forum.

However, more ways to offset the wellness inequities in our culture have to be addressed. They do include the Kawartha Loon. The local Health *(handwritten at top)* Converted it to online currency

Unit, through Nourish issues a coupon to buy local food seemingly with no understanding that the Kawartha Loon is a fully monetized complementary currency to the Canadian dollar and is purchased at a discount. This is but one example of the failure of the local community (in this case including the Health Unit and Transition Town) to work together focused on a common goal, be it food and wellness security or adding everything together and building a more resilient community.

The Health Unit has proven to be critical during this COVID-19 pandemic but does not have a clear enough mandate, operating system, or funding to overcome the social and economic inequities that can drive a 50% local food initiative or even a wellness initiative in support of local wellness providers.

Transition Town Peterborough wellness initiatives have included the Transition Skills Forum, its two festivals spring and fall and the KL local currency. It is not enough community support to establish that personal wellness is needed to build community resilience.

No specific recommendations are being made at this time but vouchers in KLs could be issued to the less fortunate in the community to buy the professional wellness services.

On Culture: *(handwritten)* 1) Bridges out of Poverty

Building a more resilient community can be the driving force and focus for a more just society, with more partnering on the place and social-based projects, taking care of one another in neighbourhood groups and our community as a whole. It is the permaculture ecosystem of living with each other leaving no one behind---Black Lives Matter. Transitioning to living more resilient lifestyles in full knowledge of the disruptive nature of our fossil-fuel-driven energy and economic systems helps us to heal ourselves and reduce our carbon footprint while helping our living planet to heal for future generations.

Building our local resilience is the cultural celebration of community at two festivals each year hosted by TTP. Both were canceled in 2020 because of the COVID-19 pandemic.

However, both are planned to return in 2021. The first, close to the summer solstice, called the Peter Patch LocalPalooza reclaiming our soul and then the Purple Onion Harvest Festival celebrating local food and culture that takes place close to the autumn equinox. Both festivals are held in the downtown core in Millennium Park on the river.

Both festivals feature everything local, including local food, local artists, local music, locally owned businesses including caterers, farmers and wellness providers with everyone using the KL local currency---all to advance the celebration of our local culture.

Further, it is readily observed that we have started to pull together a cultural centre in East City around the lift lock and canal system with the Peterborough Museum close by and the new Canadian Canoe Museum soon to bring more international visitors to our city.

City planning in view of the declining retail space requirement from the trend towards online shopping needs to start to look at the underutilized buildings in the downtown core and decide the best and highest use for these buildings to help improve the vitality and economic driver role of the downtown core.

The first move would certainly be to build the replacement for the existing Memorial Centre in the downtown area. Then the underutilized Peterborough Square and Armories and the empty Bank of Montreal Building should be matched against the requirement for a more centrally located Peterborough Arts Centre, a stand-alone Peterborough Sports Hall of Fame and a community centre.

Upgraded incentives will need to be provided by the City to preserve heritage buildings in the downtown core.

what cost?

Further, a light streetcar rail system is recommended on George St. from Hilliard St. in the north through the downtown core with wider street walks and no parking from City Hall through to Sherbrooke and a two-way single rail through to Morrow Park with the return loop to Hilliard along Water St. The rail garage would be located in Morrow Park. A transportation plan such as this would connect the downtown culture centre to the important parks in the area allowing room for safe bicycle travel and would remove cars from the road, reduce emissions and encourage both private residential and commercial development along the rail route.

This would constitute Phase1--- hopefully ripping up George and Water St only once in the next ten years. Part 2 and Part 3 would extend the light rail system to Trent University and Fleming College respectively and eventually with a spur line to the regional hospital that would allow the removal of what looks like parking for a thousand SUVs that need to be removed from the area.

I. ECONOMIC LOCALIZATION INFRASTRUCTURE:

Economic localization infrastructure in all its forms is backed by the understanding that it has some permanence to it and in this case becomes a part of the permaculture operating system to create a more resilient community.

It should be no shock to most of us that there is not sufficient economic localization infrastructure in place in our Peterborough Community to drive us to the goal of becoming the most resilient community in Canada by 2030 In short, we are significantly under invested in our own community.

This situation didn't just arrive at our doorstep.

Communities all over the world find themselves in the same position.

The clear cause, in short, is globalization and international trade run on cheap fossil fuels led by global corporations and the private banking system both supported by central banks, the largest of which is the US Federal Reserve, continuing to suck much of the capital out of communities like Peterborough, often leaving them a shadow of their former state.

An economic localization infrastructure strategy is an effort to build back some of that infrastructure into the Peterborough Community to help make it more resilient and capable of supporting new family formation for continuous vitality and renewal.

Even the idea that local residents in the Peterborough Community can invest their capital in the global economy and only invest the return on that investment locally does not provide for the investment needed to build their own community resilience.

It is not uncommon for the majority of citizens and their leaders, including members of City and County Councils, to never give economic localization infrastructure a second thought and continue to invest all their personal capital outside the community in which they live.

So, the job at hand is to increase the number of economic localization infrastructure investment opportunities available in the community.

The following is a brief summary of available opportunities:

1. If we were able to set up the renewable energy trust, as in Appendix A, it would be designed to kick-start co-ops and private investment options for local large and small investors. Over the course of 10 years, it would not be unrealistic to see that fund grow to $85 million to $90 million supporting much higher direct investment opportunities for local investors.

2. The City is always capable of issuing community bonds to fund physical structures that can become economic drivers such as

the downtown replacement for the Memorial Centre and a local food hub in Morrow Park both as economic localization infrastructure. We speculate that local citizens would be happy to buy preferred shares or bonds in such facilities to speed their development.

3. The KL local currency is technically known as a fiat fractional reserve complementary currency to the Canadian dollar---a perfectly legal entry into local monetary policy. The electronic version can be developed quite quickly at a reasonable cost and the issuer can be changed from Transition Town Peterborough to the City of Peterborough or the City and County of Peterborough or the Expanded Peterborough Trust as put forward in Appendix A. With the KL local currency as part of the trust with annual contributions by the City of Peterborough, what you have is a near bank capable of offering the foundational opportunity to become the most resilient community in Canada by 2030. Transition Town Peterborough will make a funding proposal this year to create and implement the electronic KL with the option to pass the currency issuer from TTP to an Expanded Peterborough Trust.

4. A local business investment fund would be an ideal way to allow small and medium investments in locally owned businesses and in some cases ensure generational control of some to proceed without negatively impacting the business. At this point, we know of no organization willing to step forward to organize and develop such a fund. Transition Town Peterborough has started to collect a list of strategic accounts in the City and County as possible candidates for such a fund.

J. ENVIRONMENT:

"We have to realize that cutting back emissions of greenhouse gases is only part of what we have to do; we also have to stop

using the land surface as if it was ours alone. It is not: it belongs to the community of ecosystems that serve all life by regulating the climate and chemical composition of the Earth." (The Revenge of GAIA, James Lovelock, 2006)

"Not as sexy to policymakers, but free of cost is Mother Nature's low-tech approach: photosynthesis and the buildup in the soil that naturally follows. And therein lies our great green hope. To be sure, we must continue to cut back on fossil fuel use and needless energy-squandering lives. But we also have to extract excess carbon from the atmosphere by working with photosynthesis instead of against it. Farmers, land managers, city planners, and even people with backyards have to make sure plants are growing vigorously, without large stretches of bare earth - photosynthesis can't happen on bare earth. We have to take care of the billions of microbes and fungi that interact with the plant's roots and turn carbon sugars into carbon-rich humus. And we have to protect that humus from erosion by wind, rain, unwise development, and other disturbances." (The Soil Will Save Us, Kristin Ohlson, 2014.

"By massively taking land to feed people and by fouling the air and water, we are hampering Gaia's ability to regulate the Earth's climate and chemistry, and if we continue to do it we are in danger of extinction" (The Revenge of GAIA, James Lovelock, 2006.

The TTP model has always been focused on adaptation to the climate crisis emergency rather than mitigation per se. The movement has always supported the environmental movement's drive for emission reductions while not losing sight of the need to focus on the energy descent required to build local resilience. This focus has led to the support of projects that reduce the total amount of energy consumed in all its forms while also reducing carbon emissions over the life of the project. The reverse is not always possible.

The TTP agriculture direction has always been the development of permaculture farms and food forests, which are extrapolations of the permaculture design system, while so-called regenerative farming has become a branch of permaculture farming.

All the local environmental groups utilize the TTP festival platforms and are continuously invited to take charge of some events within the Festivals.

Transition Town Peterborough is moving this year to develop one local small-scale permaculture farm as a demonstration teaching project to reduce farming emissions, build farm resilience and at the same time produce a competitive yield versus conventional farming at a lower cost.

K. SOCIAL & ECONOMIC EQUITY:

We know that we fail as a community if we leave anyone behind. Social and economic equity has to be routinely built into every project and program. This is the challenge we face as a community to drive towards building a much more resilient community by 2030.

A move towards energy co-ops, farmers' co-ops and worker co-ops is a move towards greater economic equity.

Focus on 50% Local Food 2030 is a move to provide healthier food to lower-income families and to provide many more jobs in the local food supply chain than currently exist in the industrial farming supply chain while making all citizens much more food secure.

Securing our renewable energy sources offers the opportunity for small investors to take pride in their own community and invest in their own energy security.

Issuing community bonds or preferred shares RRSP qualified for a modern zero-carbon facility to replace the current Memorial Centre will make local sports fans proud and get the building built more quickly while increasing average attendance to the games and entertainment venues.

Introducing small amounts of matching grants to neighbourhoods to replace areas with sponge gardens will help relieve the pressure on storm sewer replacement and long-term costs of water treatment.

The City of Peterborough's current project grant and investment grant funding budget can be rolled into the new trust or fund as part of the City's annual contribution with a much more equitable distribution of grants across the 4 E's.

A community centre in the downtown core to be run by a workers' co-op would provide cost-effective space for independent organizations such as TTP, other environmental groups and clubs to leverage community volunteerism against the goal of becoming a more resilient community.

L. 10 KEY ACTIONS ON THE RESILIENCY TIMELINE:

1. Declare the goal of making the Peterborough Community the most Resilient Community in Canada by 2030. Alliance required with City and County and adjoining townships and First Nations.

2. Adopt permaculture as the decision-making operating system within the 4 E's Framework (energy, economy, environment, equity) and focus on the security of life essentials. Alliance required with City and County and adjoining townships and First Nations.

3. After consultation with City Council and the County warden, the City mayor is recommended to announce the strategy of building economic localization infrastructure to pursue the goal

of a more resilient community in response to the climate crisis emergency and the COVID-19 recovery.

4. At the same time, the downtown DBIA Area needs to be communicated as the heart & soul of the community and the economic driver for the Peterborough Community and therefore the place for significant investment as we proceed to build greater resilience with more local sustainable jobs.

A more vibrant and resilient downtown area will attract more private investment and greater opportunity to promote the City as a regional tourist destination. As a destination, the downtown will be developed into a local food culinary hub which will not only attract tourists but also help to boost food security in the community as a whole.

5. City Council decides the disposition of funds from the sale of PDI to Hydro One: estimated at $50 million to $55 million.

6. City Council leads the request to re-open negotiations towards the annexation of land from Cavan Monaghan Township to be serviced for industrial/commercial development and new job creation to help solve the area jobs crisis.

7. City Council and County Council together decide to invest 1.1% of their respective operating budgets rising to 2.0% by 2030 to support the funding of non-capital projects in support of building a more resilient community by 2030.

This decision should be accompanied by a decision regarding the administrative structure of the funds, such as the trust as recommended herein to guarantee the equitable non-political distribution of funds between the City and County and in balance across the 4 E's Framework.

8. City Council and County Council to adopt the goal of achieving 50% local food by 2030. The goal is to be accompanied by

granting the coordinating leadership of the 50% local food project to PKED along with the resource funding sufficient enough to be effective.

9. PKED with budgeted local food leadership in place should convene a community task force to create the concept/feasibility/prime location of a local food hub as a major economic driver against the goal of achieving 50% local food by 2030.

10. The City and County of Peterborough are encouraged to understand the power of the economic multiplier effect in our community in support of locally owned businesses to compete with global corporations. The community economic multiplier effect could be leveraged significantly with the support of the City and County to finance the creation of the Electronic Kawartha Loon (eKL) and its actual acceptance for payment of some municipal services such as water, and park rentals and even partial payment of property taxes, etc.

If the KL local currency were to become a part of a city/county trust as originally conceived in its introduction, some of the trust fund grants could be made with a percentage in Kawartha Loons.

It is after all real money in every sense of the word developed as a means of exchange and an increasing store of value as we build to a more Resilient Community by 2030.

M. ATTACHED APPENDIX:

A. Renewable Power Generation Investment Trust Fund

(Reference Chapter 3 for this complete document)

B. Now is the Time! COVID-19 and the Climate Crisis Emergency

(Reference Chapter 1 for this complete document)

Terms & References used in this Document:

Transition Towns: refers to the international Transition Towns Network founded by Rob Hopkins in 2005.

Transition Town Peterborough (TTP): refers to the Transition Town Peterborough initiative founded in 2007 as Canada's First Transition Town.

ROI: Return on investment

EROEI: Energy return on energy investment

Fracked Oil: The correct name is tight oil from hydraulic fracturing.

Nemawashi: Japanese process of gaining support and consensus to move projects forward smoothly.

Resilient Community Measures: Some measures are posted on the TTP website and were attached to the Renewable Power Generation Investment Trust Fund Concept Proposal.

GDP: Gross domestic product, a measure of economic growth.

Energy Descent: Refers to per capita usage of all forms of energy.

Team Transition: info@transitiontownpeterborough.ca

CHAPTER 5 ▰▰▰▰▰▰▰▰
THINK RESILIENCE

THINK RESILIENCE STRATEGY PROPOSAL:

Submitted to the City & County of Peterborough COVID-19 Economic Recovery Task Force

July 20, 2020

To the City & County of Peterborough through the COVID-19 Economic Recovery Task Force with respect to the strategy towards building community resilience in the Peterborough Community to 2030 including the goal, operating system, framework, measurement, life essentials focus and requirements to ensure the most favourable outcomes for its citizens.

Context:

As presented in the Strategic Roadmap document prepared by Transition Town Peterborough and submitted to the City mayor, County warden, individual City and County councillors and First Nations chiefs in early July 2020. This strategy proposal embraces a way forward to deal with the climate crisis emergency as declared by the City of Peterborough; and other crises and predicaments including COVID-19 economic recovery, systemic racism inequities, local livelihoods, food insecurity and economic recession all of which are of major concern across the City and County of Peterborough.

Creating a Goal:

The City & County of Peterborough jointly agree to Think Resilience and set the goal, on behalf of all of its citizens, to strive to become the most Resilient Community in Canada by 2030; the date identified by the IPCC as the tipping point for many of the worst effects of the global climate crisis.

Measuring Progress against the Goal:

The City & County of Peterborough agree to delegate preparing the final measurement criteria for resilient communities and the setting of goals for the Peterborough Community jointly to the City's Peterborough Environmental Advisory Committee and Transition Town Peterborough for City and County approval within 90 days of approval of this document.

Operating System and 4 E's Framework:

The City and County of Peterborough jointly agree to accept the permaculture operating system and the 4 E's Framework as the fundamental modus operandi for guiding the decision-making process for both capital and operational funding on the timeline to creating a more Resilient Peterborough Community by 2030.

Life Essentials:

The lack of global and local progress on the climate crisis compounded by COVID-19 and other local crises has significantly heightened the need to focus on the security of life essentials including our food, water, energy, culture and wellness as our number one resiliency building priority along the timeline to 2030.

Affordable housing is arguably a life essential as well as internet connectivity. Both are part of energy in this life essentials model.

The City and County of Peterborough jointly agree to accept food, water, energy, culture and wellness as the life essentials to refine our focus and financial support in our efforts to build a more Resilient Peterborough Community by 2030.

Requirements for Most Favourable Outcomes:

A community-wide effort across the City and County including adjoining townships and First Nations and the Villages of Millbrook and Lakefield with everyone working together and leveraging all expenditures for maximum return.

A City and County zero-based crisis budgeting process to keep annual tax increases as low as possible each year to 2030.

A City and County long-term to 2030 annual operational funding budgetary commitment and a politically independent management structure dedicated to balance in the 4 E's Framework, equity between the City and County, and continuous focus on the security of life essentials.

Securing life essentials is paramount to any community resilience strategy. It is a budgetary understanding that funding for the security of life essentials can only be compared to funding for our essential workers, including police, fire, ambulance, bus drivers, healthcare workers and teachers to name some of the most prominent.

COVID-19 provides a live demonstration that not budgeting for the security of life essentials can lead to social and economic disruption beginning with our essential workers. We cannot budget for essential workers and ignore their life-essential requirements needed to protect the rest of us.

Exhibit 1 Expansion of Terms:

Peterborough Community: Includes the City of Peterborough and adjoining townships and First Nations in the County of Peterborough, including the Villages of Millbrook and Lakefield.

IPCC: Intergovernmental Panel on Climate Change, United Nations

2030 Tipping Point: Identified by the IPCC as the point of no return for holding the global rise in temperature to 1.5°C. Many parts of the world have already exceeded this tipping point, including the Canadian Arctic, increasingly affecting the weather patterns in the Peterborough area.

Permaculture Operating System: Permaculture is a system of agriculture and social design principles around the way we grow our food and live, utilizing the patterns and features observed in natural systems. Permaculture principles are the most significant in the human design for security of life essentials, including the air we breathe, the food, water, and energy we consume supporting our wellness and culture.

The 4 E's Framework: The framework references E for Energy, E for Economy, E for Environment, and E for Equity, both social and economic.

The permaculture operating system works in balance across each of the four E's and at the same time noting the connections before decisions are made. The E for Equity should not be equated to Equality.

Operational Funding: This strategy does apply to capital funding as well; however, this proposal is specifically focused to lead to setting up the operational funding needed to leverage a community-wide effort to build community resilience.

A number of capital projects are suggested in the strategic roadmap presented to City and County Council for their respective consideration.

Politically Independent Management Structure: The climate crisis emergency using the 4 E's Framework suggests the need for a separate entity to leverage the community-wide effort to build community resilience.

Firstly, the County has to be engaged in everything.

E for Energy: Peterborough Holdings is devoted to E for energy and City water.

E for Economy: PKED is devoted to E for Economy with the City & County in partnership.

E for Environment: Is not given equitable attention in either the City or County.

E for Equity: The social and economic inequity in our society is on a trajectory to overwhelm everything else if constructive actions and structure at all levels of government are not put in place to build much greater and equitable community resilience.

Exhibit 2 Sample Measures of Community Resilience:

Fossil Fuel Emissions: Per capita carbon footprint

Energy Descent: Year-over-year per-capita electric energy used

Energy Security: % electricity consumed--- locally generated

% households with on-site renewable power generation systems

% commercial buildings with on-site renewable power generation systems

% households at 80% or greater of minimum energy usage rating

Food Security: % restaurant and home food consumption grown locally

% households with pollinator and food gardens replacing lawns

	% households with rainwater collection systems
Water Security:	% Peterborough households on City water supply
Storm Water Mgmt:	% households with sponge driveways
Local Jobs:	% of local jobs in locally owned businesses
	% of local jobs in GEM: government, education, medical
Public Transportation:	% of working population regularly utilizing public transportation to and from work
Walk, Bike, eBike:	% of working population regularly commuting to and from work this way
Volunteerism:	% of population over 18 years that volunteer in the community

Community Wellness Rating: to be determined

Community Equity Rating: to be determined

THINK RESILIENCE PROPOSAL VIDEO PRESENTATION OUTLINE:

A. Introduction:

The original proposal made and distributed July 20, 2020, directly to the executive of the COVID-19 Economic Recovery Task Force chaired by the City of Peterborough Mayor and County of Peterborough Warden asks for the City and County to come together as One Community and to create the goal of becoming the most Resilient Community in

Canada by 2030, the date identified by the IPCC as the tipping point for many of the worst effects of the global climate crisis emergency.

It further advanced the request for approval of both the City and County to utilize permaculture as their operating system supported by the Transition Towns 4 E's Framework and focus on the security of life essentials: air, food, water, energy, culture and wellness.

This community-supported proposal below calls for immediate action. We welcome the opportunity to respond to all your questions.

Transition Town Peterborough Inc.

B. The Disruptors:

COVID-19 Pandemic: risk to everyone's health and wellness.

Climate Crisis Emergency: fossil fuel pollution increasing health risk, heating the planet, causing catastrophic climate events, disrupting the security of our food, water and energy supply chains.

Global Recession Local Jobs Crisis: Rising social, gender, racial and economic inequity, all of the disruptors, impact the less fortunate, women more than men and people of colour even more. It is starting to look like 30% to 40% of the population, even with our health and welfare safety nets, thus heightening the need to get moving more deliberately with equity both social and economic.

C. Disruptor Triage:

Scientific evidence clearly links climate change to habitat destruction and the encroaching loss of many species causing much greater human exposure to viruses such as the coronavirus. Scientifically, we should expect more of such viruses such as we expect more floods, forest fires, hurricanes and increased acidification and rising levels of our oceans as the planet heats up.

RE COVID-19 From Our Southern Neighbour

> *"America would be wise to help reverse the ruination of the natural world, a process that continues to shunt animal diseases into human bodies. It should strive to prevent sickness instead of profiting from it. It should build a health-care system that prizes resilience over brittle efficiency"* (Ed Yong, The Atlantic, September 2020).

Disruptor Triage Leads directly to the Climate Change Emergency:

Everyone is seriously affected, although not equally; system approach with equity, both social and economic is the only way forward.

We are running out of time to bend the curve towards significantly greater community resilience.

Building Resilience and Security in Life Essentials:

Life essentials triage leads to the focus on local security of our food, water and energy (with our economic and social culture and wellness as outcomes); and to the more rapid reduction of fossil fuel polluting emissions in the air we breathe to increase our local health and wellness.

All compounding the urgency for a much greater focus on building economic localization infrastructure by all available means.

D. Now is the Time!

- For the City and County to invest aggressively to leverage local investment in local food security and local energy security and the Third Industrial Revolution that reduces the total amount of energy used and switches locally to near zero marginal cost renewable sources of energy while cutting local polluting fossil fuel emissions affecting the health of every local citizen.

- To invest where the jobs will be in the new economy... the local food supply chain, the local energy descent supply chain (both residential and commercial), the local near-zero-cost renewable energy service sector linked to the smart grid and the Third Industrial Revolution high-tech sector with the internet linking everything to everything else, every-when and everywhere.

- For the City & County to set up public funding at arm's length from the political process to maximize the leverage directly from its own citizens and its own locally owned businesses and farming enterprises.

- For the City & County to embrace both social & economic Equity in balance in all of its programs in E–Energy, E–Economic and E–Environment.

The Transition Town Peterborough Proposal, titled "Renewable Power Generation Investment Trust Fund" proposes this to kick-start investment in local renewable power generation at the commercial level.

A Transition Town Peterborough Proposal on City & County Municipal Operational Funding for 2021 will follow this Systems Framework Proposal designed to bring the community together and working together for the common good.

E. Coming Together Around A Shared Goal To become the Most Resilient Community in Canada by 2030

- City and County on everything but most critically on jobs, energy security, local food security and the building of economic localization infrastructure.

- Locally owned businesses, including local renewable energy service companies, with local food farmers building local economic infrastructure.

- The GEM Sector leading the way in developing renewable power generation companies and a local small investor culture.

- Citizens at large, locally owned businesses and the NFP sector leveraging Municipal funding for timely solutions at a much lower cost and wider community support.

F. Measuring Progress Against the GOAL:

Becomes a unifying and liberating process in building community when following:

- the permaculture operating system

- the 4 E's Framework of energy, economic, environment, equity

- the security of life essentials

Reducing community emissions stays as job one, but there are many progressive measures along the way that are needed to focus our efforts.

Even turning the Greater Peterborough Area into a carbon sink through photosynthesis has to be a part of the resiliency plan for Peterborough.

Developing Resilient Community Measures

The Think Resilience Strategy Proposal shows sample measures of community resilience and suggests that the PEAC and Transition Town work on those measures together and submit for approval within 90 days of the Think Resilience Proposal Approval.

G. Permaculture Operating System:

It is not sufficient to declare a climate change emergency and settle for the use of a climate change lens in Municipal decision making.

Such a lens does not lead to comprehensive municipal action and funding to bring everyone together working on the same goal of building the most Resilient Community in Canada by 2030.

Using the natural permaculture system of thinking with values, ethics and design as our operating system to build a more Resilient Peterborough integrates everything with everything else making sense to new ways to live and the balancing of the 4 E's Framework, and strategic focus on life essentials.

H. 4 E's Framework:

The 4 E's Framework is needed to bring balance to our collective responses on our way to the most resilient community in Canada by 2030. It doesn't mean that our investment in each of the E's will be the same, but rather that they all must be dealt with at the same time with as much social and economic equity as we can muster.

E for Energy:

Energy is the driver of our way of life and the cause of the major climate crisis disruption. It has to be dealt with first and foremost with major investment.

Re Jobs from now until 2030---the local energy sector and local food sectors will predictably be the major local job producers. Transition Town Peterborough would be pleased to work with the City and County and/or PKED and with the Trent Community Research Centre to verify.

Not to diminish the high-tech sector moving us deep into the Third Industrial Revolution and the marginal cost economy by 2030.

Energy Descent: Our laser focus has to be on energy descent on a per capita basis no matter the source of that energy. This assertion is based on years of analysis of the very high EROEI of a barrel of oil compared to all renewable sources of energy. Reference the "Strategic Roadmap for A More Resilient Peterborough Community" as posted on the Transition Town Peterborough Website.

Transition Town Peterborough has a proven energy descent residential proposal named "The Transition Neighbourhoods Project" utilizing peer-to-peer behavioural economics. This project will be presented to the City and County of Peterborough as soon as an operational fund for the climate change crisis is set up.

Switching to Local Renewable Sources of Energy: Major initiatives required to support a new local energy regime of distributive marginal cost renewable energy powered by the internet feeding two way into the smart grid have been shown for the GEM and commercial buildings in the "Renewable Power Generation Investment Trust Proposal" as posted on the Transition Town Peterborough website.

The residential light commercial sector is more difficult to leverage into the new local energy regime of distributive marginal renewable energy.

A three-level process underway in residential and light commercial built stock retrofits must be funded by all three levels of government.

Level 1: With an energy audit. Insulate, high-efficiency windows and doors, automated thermostats, heat recovery ventilators, high-efficiency appliances, heating and cooling.

This is where we are now. However, there is little or no evidence that these increases in energy efficiency actually reduce per capita energy consumption because of the addition of more and more high-efficiency appliances and charging devices including computers, smart phones, iPads, hearing aids, and the escalating time usage on the internet and now 5G in every household. It is well-known that people with highly efficient gasoline cars drive significantly more... and those with electric cars are motivated to do the same.

The Transition Neighbourhoods Project is designed for energy descent at the household level and moves our behaviour towards Level 2. The assumption that we can move to electricity in our households and with our transportation and maintain our current lifestyle is not supportable by any objective analysis that considers EROEI as outlined in the Strategic Roadmap.

Level 2: Switching out natural gas, propane and oil furnaces in the City and County of Peterborough... perhaps 75% by 2030 to electric furnaces and heat pumps, wood, geothermal, solar and wind. Primarily electric furnaces and heat pumps in the City. Level 2 will begin the escalation of residential retrofits to accommodate electric vehicle charging in preparation for the smart grid.

This is a huge undertaking requiring significant incentives from all three levels of government.

Level 3: Designing new build and retrofitting existing Built stock to become a positive source of energy to the smart grid after looking after their own electricity requirements for the building and to charge their own electric vehicles. This exemplifies the Third Industrial Revolution distributive smart grid in full operation.

No one knows what percentage of residential light commercial stock would be needed to make the Peterborough Community 100% energy secure; however, Peterborough Holdings Power Generation Division as a renewable energy service company should be able to advise City Council on the number of locally built units that are on the Micro-Fit program and coming off that program around 2030. They should also be positioned to help the City with planning new residential subdivisions to prepare for much greater power generation at the local housing level---how about south-facing roofs on 80% of the units in each subdivision.

Twenty years into the 21st century and at least ten years into the Third Industrial Revolution distributive marginal cost energy regime kick-started in Ontario by the FIT and Micro-Fit programs. It's almost as if we have no understanding as a community what these programs were intended to do, so we continue to build obsolete residential and light commercial buildings all over the City and County.

That approval practice needs to stop as soon as possible.

E for Economy:

The COVID-19 pandemic will have permanently closed out many locally owned businesses, and the combination of that pandemic with another record hot summer has marginalized many local farmers selling into the local food market. The Peterborough downtown provides visible proof of the devastation of the heart and soul of our community.

Our economic focus has to be on building economic localization infrastructure to revitalize the local economy.

In the "Transition" documentation, including in the Strategic Roadmap, the following are the key areas of investment in our own community and the major new permanent job creators:

1. Green-Energy Bonds Market: GEM and commercial renewable power generation companies for small to medium investors as outlined in our trust proposal (refer to Chapter 3).

2. 150% Local Food 2030: project as outlined in the Strategic Roadmap (refer to Chapter 4) with leadership recommended to be moved to PKED starting with this 2021 budget cycle.

   TTP commissioned and signed off a Trent Community Research Centre (TCRC) report on food insecurity in the Peterborough area. This report is posted on the TTP website.

   TTP has recently posted a new project with TCRC, titled "50% Local Food 2030 Economic Impact and Supply Chain Requirements" (both economic and physical infrastructure requirements). This project posting is on the TCRC website.

   This project is critical to local food security by the end of this decade. The City and PKED should be budgeting for what lies ahead starting in 2021.

3. Residential light commercial retrofits moving to the smart grid, net positive flow of renewables, including charging own electric vehicles within 2 to 4 years.

   Three levels of retrofits are spelled out above. Many service companies are needed to do this work creating many more quality small business jobs.

   If the City and County doesn't move quickly to support this local sector, crews from larger energy service companies outside Peterborough Area will fill the gap.

4. Revitalizing Downtown Peterborough: The downtown is the heart and soul of the community. It has taken a significant hit from the COVID-19 pandemic.

   It's a new game now, meaning that permanent recovery of the downtown has to include building the new replacement for the Memorial Centre there and the purchase of key underutilized buildings by the city signaling to commercial real estate developers that the City has serious revitalization plans in place.

   And, in this new renewable energy era, it would be a missed opportunity to not go to an electric rail system through the downtown core powered by locally generated clean near-zero marginal cost renewable energy.

5. Leveraging the Local Economic Multiplier Effect: How can you get more money circulating in the community to increase the economic multiplier effect and create more jobs?

   Nearly every large company increases their own economic multiplier effect with Loyalty Programs.

   Canadian Tire Corp. started with the Canadian Tire printed coupons and have now evolved that program into a full-fledged

Loyalty Program for purchases in company-owned stores, including Canadian Tire, Sport Chek and Mark's.

Likewise, Loblaws, No Frills, Independent and Shoppers have the Optimum Card.

What good Canadian doesn't carry one or both of these cards?

But both of these huge Canadian Companies cause the same damage to our local economy that the other local big-box retailers do, and Costco and Walmart are the two largest retail stores draining capital from this community.

That's right, they hollow-out the community and reduce the number of jobs in the community and the average pay in the remaining jobs---all supportable facts.

COVID-19 has devastated the use of paper currency, including the Kawartha Loon.

But the Kawartha Loon is a fully legal complementary currency to the Canadian dollar that can be turned into an electronic loyalty program for only locally owned businesses and farming enterprises easily transferring around the community at zero marginal cost from smartphone to smartphone.

Transition Town Peterborough has the software license and will bring this project forward for funding to the City and County.

E for Environment:

Action: Lower our carbon footprint by getting off fossil fuels as quickly as possible.

1. Leverage PDI $50 capital funds into a new renewable energy regime that leads to local job creation and local economic infrastructure for small investors.

2. From the operational fund, provide incentives to residential and light commercial built stock as above in E---Energy Level 2 to switch out natural gas, propane and oil furnaces to electric, wood, geothermal, solar and wind.

3. From the operational fund, provide funding to leverage Citizen and NFP led initiatives in applying the permaculture operating system in support of permaculture gardens, food forests, pollinator gardens, community gardens, sponge driveways, green spaces, water resources and conservation, our natural canopy and initiatives that remove pollutants of all types from the air, our workplaces, and residences.

E for Equity:

We do need gender and racial equality; however, within the permaculture system framework, we strive for social and economic equity.

The 4 E's Framework is intended to give balance and depth of understanding that we are all on the same spaceship called Earth and the more people we leave behind the less we are able to advance as one... starting here in our place in the Peter Patch that we call home.

There are many program considerations, such as a guaranteed annual income, that fall far outside Municipal control.

There are other social equity initiatives that are already funded by local municipalities, charities and clubs throughout the area. This Framework, including equity, is not intended to change any of that except through encouraging all of these entities with capital assets to divest from fossil fuels and to invest in the new local renewable energy regime.

The operational fund should be made available for issues of equity that also impact our energy, our local economy and our environment.

I. Focusing On Life Essentials:

Air, food, water, energy, culture, wellness

Firstly, dealing with air, energy and wellness, our focus is on fast-tracking fossil fuel reduction to 2030 by introducing a new renewable energy regime and switching out fossil fuels for heating in our homes and businesses. This provides a significant benefit of removing pollutants from the air improving personal and community wellness, and long-term taking pressure off our health care system.

Local energy security can only arrive when local renewable energy as a contributor to the smart grid exceeds our basic electricity emergency needs.

Secondly, dealing with food, water and energy and culture, our focus is to fast-track local food production to 2030 for local farmers to supply 50% of purchased local food for local home and restaurant consumption.

Transition Town Peterborough is active in promoting local food and has multiple unfunded projects to help move the community to the 2030 goal.

Transition Town Peterborough also opened a Trent Community Research Project titled "50% Local Food 2030 Economic Impact Analysis and Supply Chain Requirements" posted on the TCRC website.

The 50% amount coupled with non-monetized food for personal consumption including from home and community gardens, food forests, etc., will give the Peterborough Community a significant increase in food security by 2030.

The Sustainable Peterborough Plan to supply 100% of its own food by the mid-2030s needs to remain the community goal.

Thirdly, dealing with water, our supply is far from secure from flooding and impurities and the Curve Lake First Nation does not have adequate access to clean drinking water.

Finally, our culture is already deep into the marginal cost economy of the third Industrial Revolution; with the exception of our industrial food supply where prices are rising quickly from the effects of the climate change crisis; and our not yet developed local renewable energy regime proposed with the investment of the funds from the sale of PDI. To make both of the transitions--- local food and distributive renewable energy---requires the economic localization infrastructure outlined herein.

Thank you for listening to our presentation of the Think Resilience Strategy Proposal.

COMMENTARY ON THE STRATEGY PROPOSAL:

Late December 2020: The proposal was recognized by the mayor directly to me a few days after it was received. It was also recognized by County staff by return email and they were prepared to schedule a virtual time slot for the representation to County Council. A telephone interview was to be set up with the City mayor. Communications with the mayor's secretary were not successful as the annual municipal budget cycle seemed to take over. The actual video was never produced. It would have included three 4 to 6 minute videos we obtained from prominent individuals in the community speaking to energy, social equity and the environment while I was to produce a backup 4 to 6 minute video on the economic localization infrastructure.

Christmas and the second wave of COVID-19 took over, the City and County 2021 budgets were approved by the respective councils. The Province of Ontario is proceeding into lockdown, while I am committed to developing the permaculture regenerative systems to build a more resilient community to 2030. That is, I will flush them out in enough detail for them to be better understood, so that we can partner with the best, most appropriate organizations and individuals and engage the community in workshops and town halls the way we did to focus on the three ResilientPtbo 2030 in-house projects: 50% Local Food 2030, the Transition Neighbourhoods Project and the Electronic Kawartha Loon (eKL) as a loyalty program for locally owned businesses.

We have strong internal support to represent the Think Resilience proposal very soon in the new year.

CHAPTER 6 ████████████████████████

ADVANCING INTO THE AGE OF RESILIENCE

COVID-19 and the raging climate emergency of the summer of 2020 marks the entry for me into what Jeremy Rifkin, author of *The Third Industrial Revolution*, calls the Age of Resilience.

THE SUSTAINABLE DEVELOPMENT MYTH:

Indeed, the Transition movement has always been about building resilience at the community level. The uncomfortable bedfellow has always been sustainability.

The environmental sustainability movement as a driving force was popularized by the global warming crusade of former US Vice President Al Gore in his first representations to the US Senate with respect to rising CO_2 levels and the connection to rising global temperatures. He further strengthened his crusade by his book, first published in 2007, and movie titled *The Inconvenient Truth*. The science of human-induced global warming has been submitted to much discussion from supporters and deniers and continues to this day albeit with increasingly less credible support for the deniers.

The science behind Al Gore's representations was always a little less specific than portrayed but over time became more and more observable and scientifically certain as reported by the United Nations IPCC. The IPCC reports, going back to the meeting in Montreal in 2017, were able to discuss sustainability focus on mitigation and resilience on adaptation. However, the discussion always came around to what the major focus should be, namely bending the rising greenhouse gas (GHG) emissions curve downward, while in reality mitigation and adaptation should have been dancing together to the same tune.

The driving focus of the environmental sustainability movement continues to be to reduce GHG emissions by decreasing the use of all fossil fuels, most recently setting the mid-century target of zero carbon emissions.

Unfortunately for all of us, there have never been strong caveats for the goal, such as meeting the goal would require significant changes to our lifestyles and a focus on securing our life essentials; or on such inconvenient truths that the aggregate amount of energy used from all sources would have to drastically decline in order to sustain any semblance of our complex lifestyles.

Instead, the environmentally sustainable development drive proceeded into increasing the complexity of the way we live and the way we use available energy with the switch first to hybrids and then to plug-in electric cars as the leading indicator that progress was being made.

The sustainable development myth is perpetuated by none other than all the member countries of the United Nations in real and effective partnerships with global corporations and the central banks led by the US Federal Reserve, the World Bank, and the private global FIRE sector. The sole purpose is to continue the pursuit of global economic growth while setting goals for reducing GHG emissions, which are realistically unobtainable during the very energy crisis that we are now in that is the root cause of rising emissions.

In summary and in plain language, the public has been duped and misled by the global elite and our own governments into believing that we can live pretty much the way we are now without reducing the net amount of energy we use as a global civilization.

The Transition Towns movement was initiated with this understanding and its genesis started with the first-ever community-based energy descent action plan.

The global sustainable development strategy continues full speed ahead while the amount of excess energy that is required to drive economic growth is in sharp decline. We are now in the era of the end of energy growth.

This is the global energy crisis alluded to in Chapter 2 that also is the driver of the climate emergency, carrying with it continued environmental and species destruction and social and economic inequities. The social and economic inequities manifest in protesting for higher wages, the Green New Deal and the now global Black Lives Matter movement and even the backlash mob insurrection of the US Capital criminally incited by the President of the United States, Donald J. Trump.

Maybe you think that I am taking this too far. Let me quote again from Richard Heinberg's Museletter #301 of June 2017:

> *"Dealing with the end of energy growth, and therefore economic growth is the biggest political and social challenge of our time---though it's unlikely to be recognized as such (Our biggest ecological challenges consist of climate change, species extinctions and ocean acidification). The impacts of the end of growth will likely be masked by financial crashes and socio-political stresses that will rivet everyone's attention while a quiet trend churns away in the background, undoing all our assumptions and expectations about the world we humans have constructed over the past couple of centuries.*
>
> *If we're smart, we will recognize that deeper trend and adapt to it in ways that preserve the best of what we have accomplished, and make life as fulfilling as it can be for as many people*

as possible, even while the amount of energy available to us ratchets downward. We'll act to rein in population, aim for an overall population decline, so that per capita energy use does not have to decline as fast as total use. We'll act to minimize ecological disruption by protecting habitat and species. We'll make happiness, not consumption the centerpiece of economic policy.

If we are not so smart, we'll join the dinosaurs."

Forgive my repetition but once again there is no way to reduce GHG emissions on a global scale by pursuing economic growth disguised as sustainable development!

In 2021 the United Nations IPCC is the leading global body of truth on the science of climate change, continuously warning that GHG emissions have to be cut in order for us to meet the temperature rise goals by mid-century. It is not however the leading body of truth about how we would go about reducing global emissions in the midst of the energy crisis of declining excess energy which is squeezing 99% of the people on the planet in every imaginable way.

Along the same vein, resurfacing in late December 2020 in Peterborough, our local newspaper announced that two of the local not-for-profit (NFP) organizations announced the Government of Canada's financial support for them to increase local awareness of the United Nations 2030 agenda and sustainable development goal as adopted by the General Assembly in 2015. Wow, how great is that! Both of these local organizations know about the Transition Towns movement and our work on community resilience, so we will reach out to them soon.

One of the UN goals in the 2030 Agenda is to work with Indigenous Peoples. We in TTP try very hard to incorporate Indigenous thinking, values and ethics into our thinking and believe that the First Nations Peoples in our area will see through the sustainable development myth and make suggestions along the lines of listening to the land and the water and take the energy from the sun to determine a more sustainable existence; and if the river floods or changes direction, move to be in harmony with nature.

The closest that we colonizers have come to understanding Indigenous thinking, values and ethics is to incorporate permaculture as our operating system of ethics and values to live more resilient lifestyles in harmony with the natural environment. Permaculture regenerative systems are direct outcomes from the utilization of permaculture as the operating system for every official Transition Town initiative in the world. It is a requirement of all official Transition Town initiatives to have a certified permaculturist as part of their working group. In TTP our permaculturalist is a member of the board of directors as a director of permaculture operations.

Further, the United Nations 2030 Agenda has been in effect since 2015, while global GHG emissions have continued to increase over that same period, raising the appropriate and well-known saying that doing the same thing over and over again expecting different results is the definition of insanity.

We absolutely do not need the United Nations Sustainable Development Goals to 2030.

What we need is an energy descent program and the building of community resilience everywhere on earth.

THE ENERGY CRISIS ARRIVES WITH PEAK CONVENTIONAL OIL IN 2006:

My first full-time job after obtaining my undergraduate degree was in the oil industry. My lifetime road markers were service stations. I knew how much energy there was in a barrel of oil. I was an Oil Peaker on arrival into the Transition Towns movement. I knew that access to oil defined the major wars of the 20th century. I knew about shale oil, the Alberta tar sands, and deep-sea oil but totally miscalculated the global oil industry and national government cartel's determination to search for and develop unconventional sources in order to perpetuate global economic growth at all cost.

I also knew that it took a few years past the peak to realize that the peak had been reached.

According to the International Energy Agency, conventional crude oil production peaked in 2006 while the EROEI of conventional oil was already in sharp decline. As the saying goes, the industry had already picked the low-hanging fruit. New sources of oil would come at both a higher price and a much lower EROEI.

The global environmental sustainability movement continued its pressure on emissions reduction, attacking coal as the biggest culprit and forcing the conversion of much of the coal-fired power generation plants in the US to natural gas, another GHG emitter, albeit less potent than coal. The emission reduction from this conversion was less important than the reduction in airborne particulate pollutants including lead, cadmium, and carbon monoxide and volatile organic compounds (VOCs) that the sustainability movement was happy to embrace to save lives.

FRACKING FOR OIL & GAS REBOOTS ECONOMIC GROWTH:

Well before the peak of conventional oil in 2006, Big Oil and most national governments including the US and Canada were well aware that the amount of available excess energy was no longer sufficient to support economic growth with rising technological complexity and diminishing returns to the greater good of 99% of humanity. Along the way, it was well understood that you could upgrade your smartphone with more and more features and apps that were easier to use but you were already capable of reaching and following more people and more news than you ever cared to. In other words, increasing technological complexity was starting to have diminishing returns to its users and society at large.

In any event, the idea that the amount of available excess energy was becoming the major constraint to economic growth spearheaded the search for more unconventional oil. This search started with deep sea oil and Arctic oil but was soon overwhelmed by the oil and gas fracking industry in the US.

Fracking became the major source of new oil and new gas in America. However, the industry proved within its first decade to be one of very low financial return on investment and very low EROEI while accompanied by a great deal of new pollution of groundwater and methane gas release.

The fracking industry rocketed the US to a top oil producer in the world again and delayed the idea that Peak Oil, at least the peak of conventional oil, would end the idea that economic growth was dead. The fracking industry was celebrated as the saviour of economic growth and provided the recovery stimulant from the Great Recession of 2008/2009.

Much lower oil prices caused by the fracking boom started the more rapid build-out of solar and wind sources of energy to where we are today, but the build-out rate has never filled the energy gap provided by the lower EROEI of not only conventional oil, but of fracked oil and gas, deep-sea oil and tar sands oil.

In Canada, the Alberta tar sands, with perhaps the lowest EROEI resulting from the most complex system ever to gain a barrel of oil, became a factor in global oil production and a huge disruptor to both the Canadian environmental sustainability movement and Canadian national politics.

To repeat, it was the US fracking boom that moved us out of the Great Recession of 2008/2009. Economic growth was no longer dead; the energy crisis was moved to the back burner and the economy and economic growth were rocking and rolling again. This was especially true in the US but also around the globe because oil could be purchased at reasonable prices by the rest of the world. The US provided for most of its own needs and all other countries in the world needed to buy their oil monetized in the almighty US dollar.

By the time Trump entered the White House in January 2017 he was able to declare the US's oil independence and as the number one oil producer in the world. Those who followed oil knew that there was trouble in the oil patch in Saudi Arabia and in the US fracking industry, exemplified by Richard Heinberg's June 2017 quotation shown above and *Greenzine* articles in Chapter 2 herein, but nobody, including the United Nations, Wall Street, Trump or any large news organization, was telling the truth about where we were on energy.

Oil was black gold in America again! The newly elected President Trump's first foreign trip was to Saudi Arabia, the number two oil producer in the world where both countries could openly celebrate their riches. Trump ate it up! His "Make America Great Again" (MAGA) triumph was on a roll!

If you are part of the environmental sustainability movement in Canada, you believe in reducing Canada's GHG emissions by mid-century to the target point. And you are also fairly certain that we need to shut down the tar sands immediately if not sooner to achieve those goals.

To keep the country together and to stay in office, the current Liberal minority government offers up new increases in the carbon tax to stimulate the reduction of GHG. The Conservative right argues that this is on the backs of the people despite the fact that 90% of the tax is rebated to low-income Canadians who don't pay the bulk of the tax in the first place.

The carbon tax is a baby step of marginal effectiveness in terms of what we really have to do to move the human race into the age of resilience starting for us here at home in Peterborough, Ontario.

BUILDING RESILIENCE AT COMMUNITY LEVEL:

Back to Al Gore and more sobering commentary. He was successful in training many global warming crusaders around the world including in Canada and with two of such folks in Peterborough. Both of the local Gore crusaders have supported Transition Town Peterborough and have contributed to our *Greenzine* magazine and attended multiple TTP workshops and other events. The Gore Crusader focus was sustainability and advocacy at the federal and provincial government levels to implement carbon taxes as the best means to cut global emissions and most recently get off all fossil fuels as soon as possible. Meanwhile, the transition movement proceeded with the goal of building local community resilience.

Community-based resiliency building requires lots of work from lots of people with little to no protesting against the political and economic elite and with the full understanding that to become a more resilient community, lifestyles have to change and the total amount of energy consumed has to decrease. This is not to say that very often local sustainability plans and initiatives have made significant progress in changing lifestyles in the support of bicycles and walking cities, community gardens, pollinator gardens and more green space. However, emissions have continued to rise.

Indeed, the first Transition Town Peterborough initiative in 2008 named "Streets for People" engaged in supporting the conversion of front lawns into permaculture gardens. This was easily supported by both the sustainability folks who never mentioned the energy crisis or the economy as well as transitioners who had watched the early documentaries, such as Peak Oil, The End of Suburbia and Escape from Suburbia and others advocated by the Transition Towns Network.

However, the environmental sustainability local activists rarely delved into permaculture and the solutions that engaged in energy descent, economic localization infrastructure, and local food and wellness initiatives as local economic multipliers that build communities. The balanced approach to energy descent, while switching as quickly as possible to renewable sources of energy, has always been a big differentiator between the resiliency movement and the environmental sustainability movement.

Indeed, the first proposal made to the City of Peterborough by the newly minted Transition Town Peterborough group before it became a registered not-for-profit organization was to create an energy descent action plan. At the time, the new transition group had little political support and so the idea of energy descent died on the vine as a revolutionary idea with the support of only the one pre-sold councillor.

Many years passed with the City's sustainability manager regularly advising us transitioners to avoid the idea of energy descent---it just was not politically correct. Subsequent Peterborough City and County Councils up to the current ones remain misinformed about the need for energy descent.

GLOBAL ENVIRONMENTAL SUSTAINABILITY MOVEMENT HAS FAILED:

The very controversial point that has to be made is that the environmental movement supporting the idea of sustainability and cutting carbon emissions globally has essentially failed as emissions have continued to rise to over 400 equivalent parts per million. Only in the Great Recession when the price of oil reached $147 US per barrel did global emissions decline from their steep and steady rise from the invention of the steam engine fired by coal that marked the start of the First Industrial Revolution.

At this writing in early January 2021, it is too early to predict if a global COVID-19-induced recession will pervade, and if it does if it will be accompanied by a decline in carbon emissions. The seemingly obvious link of global emissions to the global economy is blurred with COVID-19 as stock markets around the world led by the US

DOW and the S&P are hovering around breaking or pushing against all-time records. How could this be? Are global stock markets now totally disconnected from the real economy where most of us live? Do these Wall Street financial wizards know something about energy and economics that we transitioners don't know or understand? We often wonder, despite Michael Bloomberg's efforts have they ever heard about the carbon bubble?

Do they know how much energy is in a barrel of oil?

And do people who invest their money in the stock market not understand, as presented in Chapter 2: Our Casino Economy, that as quoted from Robert Castanza's book *Wealth of Nature*, "Out of every dollar of value circulating in the world's human economies, something like 75 cents was provided by natural processes rather than human labor"? And oh, by the way, oil is part of the natural processes and burning it and converting it to all kinds of plastic products is killing us even while we are running out of the best high-quality oil requiring the least amount of energy to extract.

In transition, we have always understood that we were living in a casino economy, but this is now so extreme and downright inhumane. Here we have the stock market breaking records and rising with each new announcement of an approved COVID-19 vaccine while more people are dying every day in the US from the virus than died in the 9/11 attack on the World Trade Center or on the attack on Pearl Harbor by the Japanese.

And, in the US real economy where 99% of the people live, there are millions of people who are increasingly food insecure and unable to pay their rent and put food on the table for their families.

Here we have the USA, the so-called richest nation in the world and leader of the free world, with millions of its people lined up by the thousands in multiple parades of upscale cars and SUVs to receive food bank groceries for a week. The TV images of these food bank mobile parades in almost every major city in the richest country in the world pretty much says it all about the failure of our politics and focus on reducing emissions without even entertaining changes in our very complex lifestyles. America can't live like this much longer. When will the giant wake!

If you watch the TV images very closely, you will see that many of the families have not given up their smartphones for food. When we start to spot Teslas in the food-bank parade, we will also start to understand how our priorities have gone amok and how we need to understand what we have to do in the age of resilience. We cannot ignore food security and we simply cannot afford to have big corporations continue to hollow-out the economic viability of our cities, towns, and villages to further advantage the 1%. Local resilience is the only option for security, modest prosperity and some good fortune for most of us on the planet.

We simply cannot advance into the age of resilience without a more balanced approach to the climate emergency offered herein that includes both global and local economies and real energy descent everywhere.

Al Gore can't be blamed for the failure of the environmental sustainability movement over these last 15 years, although he has accumulated an amazing fortune that puts him into the 1% financially secure elite, which is easily translated into political elite power around the world. However, I haven't heard of the use of his power to move his solution focus from environmental sustainability to reducing emissions and energy descent at the local level as the much more difficult task of changing lifestyles and the building of community resilience from the bottom up.

THE PARIS CLIMATE ACCORD:

Even the most powerful global committee, the IPCC, with its Paris Climate Accord moving into legal force in 196 countries in the world on November 4, 2016, has so far been unable to change the trajectory of the rising carbon emissions curve.

The Paris Accord is an agreement to keep the global rise in temperature to 2°C by mid-century versus the start of the First Industrial Revolution and advocates the desirability of keeping the rise to 1.5°C to avoid the most devastating effects of the climate crisis. This Paris Accord speaks of the vision of improving resilience to climate change and reducing GHG emissions all in the same sentence.

This was refreshing to us transitioners around the world but not nearly soon enough to tackle the global problem of the lack of understanding of money, global capitalism, absolute energy descent to reduce emissions and the importance of life essentials---all part of the resiliency imperative. As an example, how do we break the cartels around the world between national governments and large global businesses disguised as international trade agreements that hold sovereign nations financially responsible for non-conformance? We the people can be sued but the corporations cannot be held liable, meaning that we the people have no recourse against the corporations for issues of their non-performance.

There are many, many more examples of how national governments and global corporations have green washed the environmental sustainability movement and even support the oxymoron of sustainable development---the most glaring one being the aggressive perpetuation of the myth that all we had to do is focus on reducing CO_2 emissions and we could carry on living pretty much the same way we are in the early 21st century.

We could expect increasing levels of technology to make it easier and more fun to navigate life with no consequences---just keep buying higher technology stuff---we will as a human race soon colonize the moon and eventually Mars. Even the Tony Bennett song starts that way: Fly me to the moon and let me play among the stars. OK, I know Mars is not a star!

At this point, suffice to say that the total global focus on GHG emissions and their effect on rising global temperatures has taken away from the acceptance for much greater emphasis and resources at the local level where people live and can enact the changes that will make the difference--- to our lives and livelihoods.

WILL THE US RE-JOINING THE PARIS CLIMATE ACCORD MAKE A DIFFERENCE?

I learned from a Xerox consultant in my early business career that "a difference that makes no difference is no difference." At the time it was a profound reminder for me of Peter Drucker's teachings in his multiple books on the effective executive, including the insight that most businesses focus on efficiency rather than effectiveness. Most actions in most businesses make no difference. I am suggesting that the same applies to a larger degree with respect to most government actions. They make no difference.

Certainly, the world will welcome the US back into the Paris Climate Accord with great expectations.

However, the question remains what difference will it make in terms of bending down the rising GHG emissions curve?

As I write this on January 7, 2021, the day after President Trump incited the insurrection on the US Capital, and the day after the State of Georgia elected two Democrats to the US Senate giving the Democratic Party Control of Congress and the Executive Branch, I speculate that it will make no difference to rising GHG emissions in the short term. Indeed, the two big agenda items of the incoming Biden Administration that are likely to proceed very quickly will most certainly increase emissions from the COVID-19 low in 2020.

These include a COVID-19 Recovery Package to get most everyone back to work and put food on the table for the growing number of people who are now food-insecure casualties of COVID-19. Secondly, a huge infrastructure package is designed to increase jobs and grow the economy.

President-Elect Biden wants to be in the Paris Climate Accord, however, his televised speech days before the rioters stormed the US Capital was not shy in saying that his economic policies would pursue economic growth.

The infrastructure package as announced by President-Elect Biden will include electric recharging stations across the nation and other build-outs of solar and wind power generation, but also repairing and replacing bridges and airports driven by the oil economy. There is no indication that the infrastructure package would include high-speed rail along the Boston to Washington corridor and LA to San Francisco for a start. It may be too late to even contemplate a future of high-speed rail in the US with a diminishing availability of high-quality oil at reasonable prices.

Police brutality, criminal justice reform, and health care enhancements to the Affordable Care Act are expected by Democratic Progressives, along with long-ignored immigration reform. All these social issues go to the bedrock of US society and its fundamental values. These issues will have to be dealt with to move the USA into the age of resilience. Predictably, progress at the national level will be slow and will have very little effect on bending the curve of rising GHG emissions.

By the time this extensive agenda is halfway through, the Republican Party will predictably have re-united around the idea that the Democrats are socialists and are bankrupting the country. Standby!

This notwithstanding, the Biden Administration will likely work hard with executive orders with the Paris Climate Accord as some cover to set goals for the electrification of all new car sales by 2035 and declare water a human right and reverse all of the federal regulations on air and water quality reversed by the Trump Administration from the Obama Administration's eight years of work. The Biden Administration will likely tread softly with the fracking industry's methane and groundwater pollution to keep Pennsylvania in the Democratic Party leading into the mid-term elections in 2022. The bottom line though is that President Biden might very well make better progress on climate change with executive orders than through legislation.

There are already indications of this direction with the appointment of John Kerry as his climate change czar and a member of his Cabinet. He will be able to implement executive policy without Congressional approval as Obama did during his presidency.

However, the GHG emissions that assure global temperature rise are already in the atmosphere.

On the positive side, the high-level US climate change representation by John Kerry should trigger a more committed approach for the world, dragging his own country along so to speak, and hopefully, lead to a globally supported UN humanitarian fund to help climate change victims recover from the very worst effects of climate change. It would protect the poor and less fortunate from the ravages of climate change caused by the emissions of the wealthy nations and leading to fires, floods, torrential rains, droughts, hurricanes and typhoons that create millions of climate change refugees. The original fund idea designated US $100 billion per year transferring from the rich nations to the poor nations, but that simply did not happen.

After all, John Kerry was the first senior US government official who, as a member of the Obama Administration, spoke openly in public about the Syrian Civil War being caused by the displacement of people as a result of climate change. He used the words climate change refugees to identify the mass migration of Syrian refugees to Europe and Canada and elsewhere in the world. Further, John Kerry is a seasoned negotiator who knows the United Nations and where they have strong global influence within existing treaties, particularly those pertaining to the high seas and international air transport and travel where they might very well enact small changes that have a significant impact on emissions reduction in aggregate.

I'm hoping that John Kerry and Al Gore will soon get together and start to change their messaging to include and support community resilience with a full understanding of the permaculture design system that can be applied everywhere at any scale from the bottom up.

WILL SWITCHING TO RENEWABLES SOLVE THE EMISSIONS PREDICAMENT?

The short answer to this question is not without a significant reduction in the amount of energy consumed.

This reality manifests itself in the global environmental sustainability direction perpetuated by the rich nations of the world much less than it should. The problem of course is that few people in the world support the notion that we simply cannot replace all of the current energy sources with renewable energy and carry on with business as usual. The dominant Western nations' thought process is to switch to electricity to reduce emissions, recycle, recycle, recycle, get rid of plastic straws and bags, turn your green waste into compost, change out your appliances and lighting fixtures to high-efficiency ones, buy an electric car, support planting more trees, protect the polar bears, and give me an app for that!

The commitment to increasing global and national economic growth supported by every politician in the world from the left and the right is perhaps the largest single deterrent to an orderly change from the global economics of consumption to the economics of localization and happiness that can reduce consumption of all forms of energy.

The economics of localization and happiness focuses on fulfilling all of life's essentials, including shelter, food, water, energy, culture and wellness, all at a human scale and using much less energy of all types. It is the challenge of the transition resiliency movement in Peterborough, Ontario, Canada, and around the world.

IS NUCLEAR POWER A VIABLE OPTION?

To digress a little, I believe that the science of collecting accurate data of average global temperature has improved in accuracy and consistency over the past 15 years, but I have been led to believe by either James Lovelock, the founder of the Gaia hypothesis, or James Hansen, the former NASA scientist, or maybe both that the true measures of climate change are rising sea levels and ocean acidification. Both of these scientists are heroes of mine even though they both advocate the rapid build-out of nuclear power generation as the best solution to replace fossil fuels by mid-century. The question for me is--- What am I missing?

Although my undergraduate degree is in theoretical physics from a university with an on-campus research nuclear reactor, I am nowhere nearly up-to-date on the new reactor technology to judge the technological viability of nuclear power on a global scale---despite the success of France and South Korea to name a couple of the best examples of countries that I have visited and are most aware of their respective nuclear power generation programs. A quick check reveals that approximately 70% of France's power generation is nuclear whereas in South Korea it's approximately 22%. France has plans to reduce its dependency on nuclear while South Korea's long-term plans since Japan's 2011 Fukushima power plant disaster are less clear. Both Germany and Japan continue with plans to decommission nuclear power plants because of public concerns for safety and the regulations that have been imposed as a result.

If we were to attempt to build-out nuclear power to a global scale, taking out all the enormous amount of coal-fired power generation that exists in Germany and China as an example, I simply don't see how it could be in place by 2050. The build-out alone would require huge amounts of fossil fuels causing equally huge increases in CO_2 emissions to prepare the building sites, produce the cement and steel to build them and discover and purify the rare earths and the radioactive fuel to fire them and keep them under control. It's very hard for me to contemplate how such a build-out could ever bend the GHG emissions curve downward during their useful life. Not only that, we are running out of the low-hanging fruit of mined ore that must be purified to fire nuclear reactors just as we have with conventional oil, so the technology has a built-in diminishing return equation.

This is all about nuclear EROEI. Is it both cost-effective (i.e., positive ROI) and energy effective (i.e., positive EROEI)? The ROI calculation is the easiest to arrive at but is nonetheless extremely difficult. No private enterprise in the free world would take on building out nuclear to scale without government guarantees.

And, if we were to start now, we would be starting at the end of the fracking boom, mostly in the US, which has demonstrated since the Great Recession that fracking for oil and natural gas enriches Wall Street, produces a negative ROI industry as a whole that is unsustainable, and produces a near negative EROEI by all accounts and most often pollutes local groundwater. Do we want to repeat the same scenario with nuclear? I don't think so.

However, that industry did make the USA one of the top three oil producers very quickly and the number one producer for a short period. Its major success was the transfer of billions of dollars from the US Federal Reserve (the money of all the citizens of the USA) through Wall Street to the 1% of Americans who now have 40% of the entire wealth of the USA.

Notwithstanding my nuclear skepticism as the answer to the desire for the sustainable development movement to maintain our increasingly technocratic complex lifestyles well into the future, albeit with diminishing quality of life returns for most of humanity, I do recognize recent Canadian government announcements on their support for small modular reactors (SMR).

These new types of reactors would seem to operate around the range of 300 megawatts (MW). They would have some advantages over large scale nuclear power plants in that they could be partially manufactured in factories and shipped to sites like windmills and solar panels and assembled on-site. The SMR's would space-wise fit into a high school gymnasium. If they are anywhere near cost-competitive and have a positive EROEI over their design and actual life, they could be added to the distributive renewable power regime emerging in the age of resilience.

But let's get out front on this development. My skepticism with SMR's is the same story as for large-scale nuclear power plant misinformation on at least three fronts:

Firstly, nuclear power is much safer than the public in most countries wish to accept. The public fear factor is much higher than the actual history of deaths from nuclear power plant construction and actual accidents would suggest. In fact, nuclear power has so far proven to be the safest form of large-scale centralized electric power generation; but fear of accidents trumps the safety record.

Secondly, the public remains unconvinced that the storage of the spent fuel is handled appropriately in a safe manner to diminish radioactively over 100,000 years or so. However, the issue of fuel waste storage will predictably be a key public outcry that will have to be overcome. When all else fails and when any jurisdiction begins to consider the installation of an SMR in their backyard, you can see the lawn signs popping up everywhere just as we did with large-scale wind power as it was coming of age. SMR's, except in remote locations such as for powering mining operations, the tar sands and perhaps remote and Indigenous communities in the Far North, are not likely politically acceptable.

Thirdly, comes back to the useful life of the reactors. The design life of large-scale nuclear never seems to be reached, at least on the Canadian CANDU heavy water reactors. Before the design life is reached there is talk of an unscheduled extended shutdown and refurbishing at enormous cost. Will the same situation pervade for SMR's? And what is the comparative EROEI of large-scale nuclear power generation versus SMR's and versus large- and small-scale wind and solar power?

Notwithstanding my skepticism, I can relate to the possible advantages of SMR's including that the power generation is continuous and does not require storage back up. Further, although we don't yet know how cost-wise competitive they could be, the investment size for each unit would most certainly be much smaller and capable of being funded at the local community level without government guarantees, thereby adding to the economic localization infrastructure building goals that are required to advance in the age of resilience.

In summary, the sustainability movement has most often been about mitigation of the worst effects of climate change by reducing greenhouse gas emissions at the source without ever having to think about changing the lifestyles of the people who were the major source of the emissions and reducing the net amount of all forms of energy used. That is not how it was conceived, but it is unfortunately where it has landed.

WHAT ABOUT THE HYDROGEN ECONOMY AND FUEL CELLS?

Many of our well-known car companies already manufacture and sell conventional-looking hydrogen fuel-cell electric vehicles (FCEVs). Unless you live in a very busy transportation corridor where the car remains king, you may not have noticed. That alone is revealing of at least one of the problems over the next 20 to 30 years--- namely the refueling infrastructure.

We already have the infrastructure in place for fossil fuel transportation and even if we banned the production of new fossil fuel cars by 2035, the phase-out for all of the fossil fuel cars would not be complete until sometime after 2045. There is a California executive order in place to phase out all new fossil fuel cars in that state by 2035 and California generally leads the way for mileage and emissions standards in North America.

Meanwhile, the incoming Biden Administration has already announced its economic growth and job creation strategy of aggressively building out the electric charging infrastructure and renewable power generation to support the electrification of transportation and the reduction of GHG emissions to meet the Paris Climate Accord US commitments.

The hydrogen fuel-cell electric vehicle refilling infrastructure is totally different than either fossil fuel cars or electric cars and requires a new level of safety standards to store and handle hydrogen versus gasoline. This issue can be resolved through engineering design. That is, we are learning how to handle hydrogen at the consumer level, but the costs and advantages to scale are relatively unknown.

Further, in order to produce hydrogen, you need a source of energy--hopefully renewable. However, natural gas is often used to produce hydrogen, diminishing any downstream advantage the technology might have and raising many issues that have to be resolved. Not only do we not know what the ROI and EROEI at scale are for FCEVs, but we also don't know whether, in fact, we should as a society choose to be using the diminishing amount of excess energy that we will have in 20 or 30 years to produce hydrogen to fuel transportation.

I have been confronted by multiple friends including some transitioners about why I haven't enthusiastically embraced the new hydrogen cars and economy. It seems to have a lot of futuristic appeal for lots of people---and plain old sex appeal to others!

Often the fuel source is mixed up with the fuel cell. I do make the point that I don't know a lot about it, but I can't resist asking them if they know how much energy is in a barrel of oil, and if they understand that our complex economy runs on excess energy, not the energy that comes out of the ground in the case of oil; and do they understand that excess energy is in sharp decline and have they ever heard of embedded energy or EROEI. I am starting to sound like a smart ass to myself about this stuff. But energy is part of my DNA--- from $E=MC2$ to Wall Street and back to little old Peterborough affectionately known by many locals as the Peter Patch.

MORE ON THE ENVIRONMENTAL SUSTAINABILITY MOVEMENT:

Over time, the environmental sustainability movement was hijacked or green washed by big business, State governments and universities the world over. We are hoping that the same doesn't happen to the Resiliency Imperative by anchoring the movement with the permaculture operating system as was the original driving system of the Transition Towns model.

Now we have nearly every global corporation in the world publicizing their program, most of which merely export their emissions to other countries and other companies in the supply chain to the point that no one is able to calculate the real EROEI of electric cars over their useful life. Indeed, many of the advances have been to increase efficiency rather than reduce complexity.

I remember in the first few years of Transition Town Peterborough supporting international Earth Hour to bring attention to the need to cut our use of electrical energy no matter its source.

We had a team of three transitioners with the support of one City councillor calling on many of the local businesses directly for their support to shut off their lights for one hour. At the time we thought it would become a great demonstration for energy descent.

We found out a lot of stuff from that small initiative. For one, many of the local fast-food joints didn't even have control of their own electric power control box---we would have to talk to their head office! And some of the larger big-box store managers had better rates to keep the security lights on all year, 24/7.

To turn them off for one hour wouldn't be worth it even as a demonstration unless everyone else was doing it!

At the time, we were so naive to think that in the era of global warming, awareness and rising energy prices, people in their homes and businesses would want to shut their lights off and even be eager to do so. We thought that in a few short years a lot of the lit signs throughout the city would automatically be shut off to save energy if not some money, but that never happened. Industry developed higher efficiency light bulbs and eventually LEDs and our buildings and businesses are more lit up than ever before.

The local public utilities unit had multiple programs to switch to high-efficiency lighting, understanding better than TTP did at the time that increases in lighting efficiency was a multiplier for more lighting in both domestic and commercial spaces and the use of more electricity not less; just as the increases in gas mileage was a multiplier for more cars on the road and an increase in the amount of gasoline consumed. We need to understand this human behaviour to be successful with any energy descent initiative. After all, the marketing folks in the big global corporations are already taking advantage of this human behaviour in the near marginal cost economy of the age of resilience brought to us through automation, robotics and the 5G Internet of Things.(IoT)

The Dark Sign By-Law draft presented by yours truly to our one supporting councillor died before getting to the full council; and the electronic signs and lighting in the Peter Patch shine every bit as bright as in every other city in North America--- not quite to the level of Tokyo, Hong Kong, Shanghai and Seoul as they were during the last decade of the 20th century during my visits to those great cities of bustling humanity.

Needless to say, the Transition Neighbourhoods Project is an energy descent initiative that practices peer-to-peer behavioural economics. We are certain that it can work in Peterborough!

Fortunately for all of us, as the sun sets on the Second Industrial Revolution driven mostly by oil, we are left with Rifkin's IoT and a near-zero marginal-cost decentralized renewable energy regime which is cost-wise competitive with centralized nuclear and gas-fired power plants.

Perhaps this is not all, as we do have the courage and conviction to carry on to build personal and community resilience, and we do have the understanding of big data and behavioural economics to help build the regenerative systems that we can bring into the new age of resilience to help secure our lives and livelihoods and our very existence.

BOUNCING FORWARD WITH PERMACULTURE INTO THE AGE OF RESILIENCE:

Resilience is often defined as the ability for individuals and communities to bounce back after disruptions such as personal tragedies, floods, hurricanes and forest fires as are raging now. Indeed, we in TTP have always relied on similar definitions for resilience as quoted often in this book from the writings of Richard Heinberg of the Post Carbon Institute.

However, COVID-19 and the raging climate emergency now demonstrate the need to actually do much better than bouncing back after major disruptions to the way we live. We have to start to think about how we can begin to bounce forward.

Why? Because bouncing back only puts us back in the same position with the same set of tools to face the next pandemic, flood, forest fire and whatever the changing climate brings. The next once-in-a-hundred-year pandemic is most certainly less than ten years away, as is the most damaging 100-year flood here in Peterborough and around the globe.

Our only answer to how we can bounce forward, moving into the age of resilience, is to adopt permaculture as our operating system for how we live in cities and towns and on farms or in the wilderness. Not everyone in the world will have the advantage of having Indigenous Nations in their midst. Here in the Peterborough, our own *Greenzine* magazine has always been headlined Peterborough City, County and First Nations.

We do not want to presume for a moment that permaculture matches the entire philosophy of our Indigenous First Nations but rather only that it gives us the best opportunity to advance into the age of resilience and to begin to live differently, in greater harmony with nature and in consideration of generations to come.

Permaculture, as presented in Chapter 4: Strategic Roadmap, puts us in motion to think Resilience in every aspect of our lives and livelihoods. And very soon we must begin the devastatingly disruptive process of moving the coastal cities of the world to higher ground to escape rising sea levels. Dangerous storm surges from more severe storms and hurricanes are sounding the alarm as is the submergence of major barrier islands that have existed for centuries.

The age of resilience is all about utilizing the best of the Second Industrial Revolution fired by oil while leaving all fossil fuels behind to protect our environment from much greater damage that will challenge our very existence.

It's about moving with systems thinking and integrated actions across all aspects of our lives and livelihoods and leaving no one behind. It's about working together, starting at the neighbourhood level and moving upward, to building resilient communities, each of which has secured its life essentials, including its food, water, energy, culture and wellness; and like a secure family unit is positioned to contribute to the greater good of state and nation to remove pollutants from the same air we breathe in our place in Peterborough in Canada and Wuhan in China.

The age of resilience cries out for the localization of life essentials. How much of our food is grown locally? How secure is our water supply from floods and storm water contamination?

How much of the energy that we consume locally is from renewable sources and generated locally? What is our local carbon footprint and are we minimizing the negative impact on our own wellness? These are but a few of the true measures of our local community resilience. These are the types of questions that have to be answered now for our children and grandchildren and their children to be secure and prosper in a much more complex living environment.

> *"Economic Localization is such an effective solution-multiplier; it boosts employment and reweaves the fabric of the community; it shrinks our ecological footprint and maximizes ecological regeneration; it increases accountability, restores the democratic process and empowers people to take control over their own lives."* (Local Futures, September 2020)

We must build on the technology of automation, robotics and the IoT which is already highly developed for the highest of profit by the likes of Amazon, Apple, Google, Microsoft, Walmart, Facebook and Twitter and many other large global corporations including in the FIRE economy (finance, insurance, real estate). We must bring that technology to the people locally through application towards building local resilience; securing first and foremost our life essentials which collectively also provide the greatest opportunity to reduce community emissions, protect lives, create many more sustainable jobs and livelihoods, and take back the soul of the community with equity and social justice.

Suddenly in 2020 the climate crisis began to bear down on us around the world starting with the raging forest fires in Australia early in the year and later to the equally devastating fires in California fueled by the gusting winds, making you wonder why anyone would ever want to rebuild there, despite the attraction of the beautiful landscape of hills and valleys.

But then most of us living outside of Alberta in Canada never quite understood why we would want to rebuild Fort McMurray after the huge fires in May 2016 turned the town into a dangerous fireball displacing over 85,000 people, destroying over 2,500 homes and creating insurance claims of $3.5 Billion Canadian.

Residents in Fort McMurray didn't want to talk about the climate crisis as the probable cause of their displacement; they just wanted to get back to their jobs working in the tar sands. How do we overcome this human behaviour? Why does the capitalistic system not encourage rebuilding differently, safer, and perhaps in a different location?

But then the folks in Fort McMurray are no different than many who live along the gulf coast of the US in hurricane alley. Some of the folks living there wait for the news to tell them the category of the incoming hurricane to decide whether or not to hunker down, board up, sandbag and wait out the storm.

This year reminded me of the stories I wrote at the start-up of Transition Town Peterborough that are lost on an old computer long since vanished to the recycle heap, adding to my horror of built-in obsolescence. In any event, one of the stories was titled "Rome is burning!" It was about global warming and what we are going to do about it. The other one was called "A frog in boiling water" and was about how to get people's attention in time to change their behaviour to get off fossil fuels and address the resiliency challenge ahead of living within our means of available energy.

To the point, after 15 years of learning and focusing on Gaia and the Transition Towns movement, I can now say with certainty: Rome is burning! It is an emergency! We, humans, are acting like frogs in hot water waiting patiently for it to boil! And that, we can do something about our predicament by bouncing forward with permaculture to build more resilient communities.

However, let's talk some more about 2020. On the good side, suddenly with COVID-19 as a SEE, people the world over began to understand that we were all in this together and we needed to soon come together around the world. The exception to this statement is none other than the United States of America, which will likely be tied- up with the internal politics of division at least for the next few years. If the US can avoid a foreign war in the Biden Administration, it may provide the window to the age of resilience and energy descent in that country.

It's quite clear that we can't wait for America. We simply have to find our way to building more resilient communities globally before we have the USA's support. The big issue is that most of all the big corporations, including big-tech, in the world that have more big data on consumer behaviour in Peterborough, Ontario, Canada, are American and they are quite content with keeping the global capitalistic system going and perpetuating the sustainable development myth.

This means that we will likely make little progress in breaking the hold that global capitalism has on the economics of localization and of happiness unless we grab hold of permaculture as our operating system, and compete with big data, 5G, and the IoT for the soul of our communities everywhere on earth.

In TTP we are anxiously awaiting the day, likely now in 2022 when we can celebrate the Peter Patch LocalPalooza with all-local food vendors, all-local entertainment, trading exclusively with the KL local currency and demonstrating the electronic version---the eKL.

For those of us who have some understanding of the climate crisis, we knew that the COVID-19 virus may have jumped from bats to humans but only because of habitat destruction caused by humans in the age now identified by anthropologists as the age of the Anthropocene.

What we are saying is if we do not choose to make this the Age of Resilience then the Age of the Anthropocene will be short-lived and will not include the era of changing lifestyles and the healing of Gaia.

The Age of Resilience leads us directly to the development of permaculture regenerative systems that move us into the economics of localization and happiness through social and economic equity.

CHAPTER 7

PERMACULTURE REGENERATIVE SYSTEMS

FOREWARD:

The Transition Towns movement here in Peterborough is not about popularizing permaculture per se or even regenerative systems with the First Nations peoples in the Peterborough Area. They already get it in spades! We colonizers simply need to listen to them and absorb what they have consistently been saying to us for generations. It's not the other way around.

What we are trying to do in the transition movement is capture the words, the language and the stories that will lead us to work together to build more resilient communities here and around the world.

Words do matter, language matters, constructively produced words such as permaculture regenerative systems can lead to living stories that can change the way we live in much greater harmony with nature.

Word constructs such as "sustainable development" giving cover to economic growth as alluded to previously in this book have set the resiliency movement at the community level back for years; while the total misunderstanding of the way our money is created and distributed throughout our society already has a generational grip on misinformation about our economics. Much of this at the top of the food chain of economics is exposed by Stephanie Kelton the author of *The Deficit Myth* copyright 2020. Much more of the economics of localization and happiness follows.

Despite the permaculture regenerative systems' deterrents manifesting from the lack of understanding of energy and its role, the myths surrounding our money and the need for economic growth, real stories are emerging all over the world that are moving us to the same resiliency imperative.

They are emerging first and most logically as environmental regenerative systems. In the Transition Towns movement, the stories from Cuba, after the Soviet Union pulled out of that country and virtually cut off its oil supply, were most instructive. The tiny nation immediately began to re-learn permaculture to feed itself without the use of fertilizers and insecticides. The word permaculture or its Spanish equivalent was never used. As a nation, they simply tapped into the knowledge of their elders and re-skilled their population on how to grow food and live differently in harmony with nature. The nation's citizens on average lost weight but they became healthier at the same time reminding us of the benefits of real food.

Early in the formation of TTP, we formed the Transition Re-Skilling Institute and utilized volunteers to teach multiple classes in permaculture and added workshops on the many skills that would be needed to become more resilient and to feed ourselves without oil. The group name was later changed to the Transition Skills Forum where volunteer workshops in normal times would be taking place today.

Ted Turner, the founder of CNN, a significant philanthropist, and the founder of Turner Enterprises presents us with one of the greatest gifts to the regenerative systems knowledge base. I don't know Ted Turner, but I am guessing that he may have never heard of the word permaculture. However, he likely knows more about the regeneration of land than most of us. Turner Enterprises owns just under 2 million acres of land in 14 ranches in Montana, Nebraska, South Dakota, New Mexico and Kansas with just under a total heard of 45,000 bison running free range on the great plains on his ranches.

The bison by now have a symbiotic relationship with the land, water and sun and other species of both plants, insects and animals, including human, as they did for over 2,000 years with the Indigenous People who prospered there.

The manure from the bison with the help of the evolved shape of their hoofs helps to regenerate the soil, attracting billions of insects, creating meadows of new grass and flower species which attract a wide variety of bird species and small mammals.

Replacing a role the Indigenous Peoples played in the food chain when they roamed and lived off these lands and fed off the bison, Turner Enterprises has opened up a chain of restaurants, Ted's Montana Grill, serving his homegrown buffalo meat and making the entire project into a viable business model.

Turning now to James Howard Kunstler, the author of *Living in the Long Emergency*. I met him when he was in Peterborough giving a presentation at Trent University where he autographed my copy of his book *The Long Emergency*. I know that he is quite familiar with the Transition Towns movement and with permaculture. As I was reading his "Portraits in Heroic Adaptation," I kept thinking that I was reading about people moving into their own constructs of permaculture regenerative systems---that was inspiring---and that is the way it should move ahead on an individual basis to build personal resilience. Many folks in the Peterborough area are doing the same thing, generally starting with permaculture or pollinator gardens and moving to reduce their own energy consumption everywhere they can. Transition Town Peterborough as part of the Transition Towns movement is engaged in scaling the building of resilience to the community level.

I also wish to make the point as observed by Howard Kunstler and reinforced in each of the stories he writes that the people in the stories are adapters, not mitigators. That is exactly what we transitioners are. We are dedicated to both personal adaptation and adapting our communities to build community resilience.

So many other TTP positions are covered so cleverly in Kunstler's new book that you will have to read it to get them all. I will just carry on with a bit more review to shed light on other areas of agreement.

We in the transition movement in Peterborough apply the use of permaculture as our operating system of design across what we call the 4 E's Interactive Framework---energy, economy, environment and equity---that must be worked in balance in order to advance into the age of resilience and to build much more human scale and resilient communities. This direction is presented in Chapter 4: Strategic Roadmap. The listing of the 4 E's in order is deliberate. Energy comes first as it has since our inception.

We are in an energy crisis of declining excess energy at a time of much greater technological complexity which is causing the real global economy where most of us live (as alluded to in Chapter 2: Our Casino Economy) to contract. The real economy is confirmed in Howard Kunstler's new book to be contracting. He does give some explanation as to why as I hope we have in this book and he does recognize in summary that "shale oil will be a shockingly short-lived miracle" as we have noted in our *Greenzine* magazine from the start of the boom in the US.

Kunstler also goes on to say that shale oil (or tite oil, the commonly used name for oil from the fracking process, which is more specifically referred to as the hydrofracking process) made the US the number one oil producer in the world, celebrated by the king of debt, President Donald J. Trump (my cynical words as Trump himself has proclaimed). However, the short-lived "miracle" is all about the industry's inability to even pay the interest on the debt backed by Wall Street and supported by the US Federal Reserve quantitative easing program.

So the energy crisis is shaking the very foundation of our economy to the point of a major reset. This was all in the pipeline before the COVID-19 pandemic hit and before the climate crisis bears down on us all with much greater severity such that there will be no place to go for many of us while many others will be added to the list of climate change refugees.

What it means for us very fortunate citizens in the Greater Peterborough Area is that we need to get on with building our own community resilience with the hope that we have until the early 2030s to put in place many of the regenerative systems that will help us bounce forward from the next major crisis.

I hate to sidetrack the environmental sustainability and sustainable development movement but in all probability, the next big crisis will be in the economy as it contracts on a global basis. In other words, if economic growth keeps slowing and continues permanently, not simply for two consecutive quarters of negative growth (which defines a technical recession) but carrying on into a depression, then you have a full-fledged economic crisis. This depression may very well happen before the carbon bubble bursts as described in Chapter 2, which will cause Wall Street to halt further investment in Big Oil and force the stranding of the oil & gas reserve assets by leaving them in the ground.

Wall Street, for so long engaging in racketeering, as vividly described by Howard Kunstler, will in my words be running for the hills and the shelter of those who live in the real economy and have built some semblance of resilience in their smaller communities.

Howard Kunstler's book leaves us with an appropriate description of what is going on with the stock market led by Wall Street. It's essentially racketeering allowing the Wall Street gang and all its enablers to keep on making money while the global economy is contracting without the aggregate economic growth required to pay off the debt, estimated by Kunstler at "about $US 240 trillion globally."

To complete the racketeering--- corporations with cash buy back their stock pushing the prices still higher and pay out larger bonuses to senior executives whose performance bonus is tied to the stock price. This is exactly what happened with much of the Trump corporate tax cut that was designed to repatriate funds from US overseas subsidiaries to increase manufacturing capacity back in the USA. That didn't happen. Rather most of the money went back into the hands of the 1% through the Wall Street racketeers.

Hopefully, President Biden will be able to claw some of that money back with increased taxes on the wealthy, but it won't affect the real economy much before a major monetary reset occurs, or in the way of reducing the interim inflationary effect on the dollar because the already rich hoard their cash and need not spend much more in the consumer economy to survive.

I also won't go into the last resort global fix of the International Monetary Fund issuing special drawing rights (SDRs) rather than facing up to a global currency crisis where the nations with fiat currencies come clean with the lack of a store of value to support their own currency. The SDR solution is another capitalistic temporary fix before total collapse.

Peterborough, like many communities all over the world, has neglected to build its own store of value. It has sold out to globalization, big banks and big corporations so much so that it will take total commitment to build community resilience to at least make some impact before the climate crisis affects everyone on the planet or before economic collapse. Both are sadly inevitable.

The way we build the store of value in the Greater Peterborough Area is through building permaculture regenerative systems with a laser focus on our life essentials, starting with securing our energy and food which provide the synergy to help us build the economic localization infrastructure needed to scale to community size. The major constraint is the local municipal government's fixation on sustainable development and GHG emissions as the response to the climate crisis and avoidance of our energy and food security and the knowledge required to build economic localization infrastructure to build much greater community resilience to the benefit of everyone.

I'm writing this section on January 15, 2021, the date of Drew Monkman's special report to the Peterborough Examiner local daily newspaper, which highlighted five months in 2020---January, March, July, November and December---that were at least 3°C warmer than the 1971-2000 average for the same months. In the same article, Drew also reported 35 days above 30°C in Peterborough in 2020 verifying that the climate crisis will not bypass us in the Peterborough Area.

Indeed, as we have indicated before, the climate emergency as declared by the City of Peterborough is already here, adding to the urgency of building much greater community resilience by tackling first and foremost our energy and then our local economic infrastructure.

ENERGY DESCENT REGENERATIVE SYSTEM:

Because we are facing an energy crisis, the energy descent regenerative systems are the most important to be implemented to create a more resilient community. These systems interact with or are components of every other regenerative system that we construct. If we need more housing, we must construct housing that uses much less energy of all types both in its construction methods and throughout its expected life and likewise with commercial buildings. As another example, if we are going to feed ourselves with permaculture local food regenerative systems then those systems must reduce the total amount of energy used versus the current system of importing the estimated 95% of our food into the Peterborough Area with its huge amount of embedded energy from industrial farming, farm equipment manufacturing, the use of insecticides and fertilizers as well as in the transportation of the food to our area.

We simply do not have enough factual data to assess what the current per capita usage of all forms of energy is in the Peterborough Area.

Our usage comes to us in so many forms: not only in our electricity, and gasoline, heating oil, natural gas and propane but in our food and almost all manufactured items including the unending array of plastic items and our clothes; and even less obvious is the embedded energy in the multitude of batteries that we purchase, without much thought, all with our collective mindset justifying their need to sustain our complex lifestyles. Nobody seems to ask just how many batteries we have in the average household in Peterborough or anywhere else in Canada! And nobody seems to know just how much energy is required to run the internet now with 5G.

However, what we do know is that Canada in 2017 had the highest per capita energy usage of major countries in the world, higher than the USA, and more than double the UK and nearly double both France and Germany. Canada as a cold country provides little rationale for its high energy consumption. Both Finland and Sweden have much lower per capita energy usage. The bottom line, as concluded by Tejvan Pettinger in October 2017, is that the huge disparity in energy use primarily reflects different income levels throughout the world. And, here we are in Canada knowingly importing most of our manufactured goods and much of our food with billions upon billions of joules of embedded energy that would make our per capita energy usage much higher, illustrating just how vulnerable we are to the carbon bubble and financial collapse and total disruption of our standard of living and lifestyles.

The Book The Energy of Slaves: Oil and The New Servitude written by Andrew Nikiforuk and published in 2012 vividly describes the amount of energy in a barrel of oil with this reference:

> "David Hughes, perhaps Canada's premier energy analyst, calculated in 2011 that one barrel of oil contains approximately 6 gigajoules (6 billion joules) or about 1,700 kilowatts of energy. A healthy individual on a bicycle or treadmill can pump out enough juice to light a 100-watt bulb, about 360,000 joules an hour. Accounting for weekends and holidays off and a

sensible 8-hour workday, Hughes figures that it would take one
person 7.37 years on a bicycle or treadmill to produce the dense,
highly portable energy now stored in one light barrel of oil. If
the person ran or rode 12 hours a day, 7 days a week, with no
holidays says Hughes, a barrel of oil would be equivalent to 3.8
years of human labor. Given that the average North American
now consumes 23.6 barrels of oil a year, every citizen employs
about 89 virtual slaves. A family of 5 commands nearly 500
slaves."

Before we carry on with the story of energy descent, we do have to link it to emissions reduction which has always been the focus of the followers of the sustainable development myth as well as the followers of environmental sustainability. Clearly, the sustainable development oxymoron being perpetuated by the national governments and global corporations everywhere on earth gives cover to the pursuit of economic growth which undermines the underlying environmental sustainability movement as a means to reduce global emissions.

The outcome of speaking out of both sides of our mouth on sustainability has led to a world where most people in the rich countries emitting most of the emissions, believe that we can continue to pursue economic growth and achieve environmental sustainability at the same time while the continuously rising emissions since the 2008/2009 Great Recession demonstrate that this is decidedly not possible.

What we are being fed by the United Nations, all the global corporations and most of the national governments of the world including Canada's Prime Minister Trudeau and US President-Elect Biden is to stop talking about economic growth, substitute sustainable development, switch to renewables and carry on with business as usual. This strategy is simply not viable in an effort to build resilient communities.

So, the point that needs to be reinforced here is that the only way to reduce emissions is to reduce per capita energy consumption. To interpret that clearly to all of the citizens in the USA and Canada is to say that we have to change our lifestyles to consume much less energy from all sources.

For any energy-decent regenerative system to actually be regenerative it must change behaviour and lifestyles.

It does remain a reasonable strategy to get off fossil fuels and aggressively switch to renewable forms of energy; however, the renewables at this point in time have no chance to replace the enormous amount of energy in a barrel of oil! And, if we choose to keep living the way we do we will soon discover that there is not enough renewable energy to replace the existing solar panels and windmills and hydroelectric plants, etc., at the end of their useful lives.

Before going too much further, I have been asked what I think of the Canadian carbon tax. I do know that the local environmental sustainability folks consider our prime minister's recent announcement to increase the tax to be a significant win. They all herald the fact that 90% of the tax is rebated proportionately by income to the people in the lowest income brackets. From a tax policy point of view, it seems to me to be a rather convoluted way by big government to transfer funds to people at the lower-income level for the bad behaviour of folks of higher income while neither group is seemingly inspired by the additional tax or the rebates to change their lifestyles and lower their per capita consumption of all types of energy.

Carbon taxes do not seem to be the mechanism needed to address the need for much more rapid energy descent at a time when the aggregate amount of excess energy for our civilization is in steep decline. The job of energy descent is much harder than that. In Canada's case, my home and native land, the tax seems to be more cover for the Canadian government to pacify the Western provinces, keep the Alberta tar sands in place, keep the country together and continue pretty much with business as usual. It also gives the national politicians and provincial premiers something to argue about that has a marginal impact on the real predicament that we are in.

The only way forward for citizens living in high-energy use countries such as Canada and the USA is to change their lifestyles to maximize their personal and community energy descent.

There are many opportunities for energy descent initiatives that impact our lifestyle or culture. Some have been implemented as a result of the environmental sustainability movement in Peterborough and most cities across Canada. These include more bicycle lanes on city streets, more bicycle trails, and more green spaces and city parks. But the migration trend of businesses to the commercial strips, providing lots of room for cars and drive-throughs continues while electric public transportation in support of higher density city centres to human scale remains totally lacking and GHG emissions keep rising.

The Transition Neighbourhoods Project is a proprietary Transition Town Peterborough project, not without the need for partnership with the City and County of Peterborough and other groups. It addresses the need for changing behaviours and lifestyles. The project is not intended to be the last of this type of initiative but is the start. It is focused on the basis of community formation, namely the neighbourhood, which is where people actually grew up and lived for generations.

My own upbringing in Brantford, Ontario, in the working-class area of East Ward is an example of a strong neighbourhood providing an extended family where everyone knew your name. It was multi-racial with different religious affiliations. We all had the same breadman and milkman deliver to our back doors every day. They both called me and my dog by name. In the winter months, as the youngest of three kids in our family, I would rush to bring in the milk to be the first to get the cream off the top of the milk bottle to put on my porridge. In the early years, the breadman and milkman delivered by horse and carriage, as did the iceman who I recall only came every three days. All the kids, boys and girls, played in the same park called Devils Half Acre. It was one city block, one block away for me.

I was one of the devils who played there well into my teens. All the dogs and cats ran wild with us kids, and we protected them from the one dog catcher in the city of 37,000---at least until the city lights came on and all the adults in the neighbourhood made us go home. You know, thinking back we even called it our neighbourhood.

The only time we would see a policeman in our neighbourhood was if there was a car accident, always at the busiest corner. We saw the police uptown, as we called it because it was uphill, I guess, but my neighbourhood seems to me now to have been self-policed.

I know this is all a fond memory from long ago but it is an example of how we have lived with much less energy. I of course grew up and delivered just over 100 of the local newspaper each day on my paper-route bicycle and collected payments once a week. I was soon adopted by those folks as their paperboy. I was never quite able to figure out what was up with two or three of my customers who rarely came to the front door when I was collecting. I eventually had to get them to pay at the office, which was a struggle. Imagine a new way to pay at a time when cash was everything.

You had to pay me, or I had to stop delivering the paper because I was buying them from the newspaper company. I became a rich kid with a regular income and glorious tips and my dad called me a capitalist because of my cash and three bicycles; one for the paper route, one for every day and one to show off. I started charging my older siblings and others to fix their bicycles.

This was the beginning for me of the understanding of good customer service, of money and accounting and running a business and the transformation of my energy through my bicycle's generator to light the road ahead.

I never quite put it together until years later as to what changed our lifestyles into the modern era, but I now know that it was the availability of cheap oil. My father was a barber, and everyone knew him or so it seemed to me. Our family got its first car in 1949 and the modern era fired by oil began for many families just like ours in Canada and the US and around the world. Little did we think in 1949 that we might someday run out of oil, the black gold that fired the modern era.

We proceed with the Transition Neighbourhoods Project (TNP) as the first specific energy descent program initiative in the Peterborough Area.

Energy descent needs to work first at the neighbourhood level then be scaled to the entire community and then to our commercial businesses to become the norm. The TNP initiative is modeled after the original Transition Streets Program that has been successfully implemented in communities around the world both smaller and larger than Peterborough. It relies on peer-to-peer behavioural economics; saving money by reducing energy at the individual household level tied directly to sourcing most of our life essentials locally and reducing complexity.

As such, the TNP is also a subset of the economic localization infrastructure regenerative system which follows in this chapter. To be regenerative the TNP has to change people's behaviour and the way people live with the available energy and reduce the consumption thereof. Hopefully, when implemented more broadly across Peterborough, it will also stimulate some people to install solar panels to cover their own needs and even become a net-positive contributor of renewable energy to the grid.

The TNP has already received modest funding from the City of Peterborough for development but funding for the pilot was not granted in the 2020 budget. COVID-19 has virtually forced us to have both hard copies and an online version going forward changing the way the program can be presented.

The other thing that is more important as we enter the age of resilience is that we need much more good data (big data) to accumulate from within the project such as housing size, square footage, construction year, lot size, R-value if available, HVAC type, fireplaces by type, window and door upgrades, types of toilets, south facing roof, water source, indoor pool, outdoor pool, fish pond, security system, electronic devices, including TV sets, etc. The City can utilize this information for planning their own and provincial and federal rebates as they arrive and for assessing the relative impact of these variables as well as to provide in whole to local companies to service the new business opportunities.

The money we have already spent on the initiative has brought us to the point that we need a paid project manager to work with an outside contractor to bring an online version together this year for use in the initial pilot and training of volunteers before the rollout in 2022 across the city and adjoining townships and First Nations. The roll-out will require at least two years with the paid project manager and a paid operations coordinator. The project manager will be the TTP director of permaculture operations maintaining the integrity of the project for its duration. Clearly, a partnership with the City and either of its surrogates, PKED or Green Up, can administer the program and pay the project manager directly; and since the volunteer coordinators are most likely to be transitioners, some already familiar with permaculture systems design, TTP might want to maintain control of the training of volunteers and be compensated for it.

The current plan is to contact PKED and Green Up by the end of February and make the proposal soon after to the City of Peterborough for funding from the Climate Change Fund of $426,000 approved in the 2021 Budget.

LOCAL RENEWABLE POWER REGENERATIVE SYSTEM:

Local renewable power generation has come to be known as distributive power generation. It involves a variety of sources of energy conversions to electricity. These include solar, wind, geothermal, small hydro, and biogas. The City of Peterborough through its public utilities commission already owns and operates solar, small hydro and biogas installations that feed into the central grid subject to the same loss of power in transmission to the point of use.

Local renewable power conversions become part of the energy descent equation for communities by the reduction of the loss of electricity in transmission. However, this only happens when we service local requirements first and feed the excess energy into the central grid thereafter. The technology to do this already exists. It's not off-grid because the same technology allows power from the central grid when needed, meaning for any installation you could be plus or minus with the grid at any time.

Beyond that, local renewable power generation is also a local economic and resiliency multiplier, increasing local jobs and increasing local energy security.

The more a community such as Peterborough builds out its own renewable power infrastructure the more it becomes secure in energy. The more that energy supports the local food and wellness sectors, the more we become resilient in these sectors to the point that citizens become aware of the economics of security, resilience and local happiness; lifestyles begin to change, and the projects become regenerative and part of the economic localization infrastructure of the community.

The Transition Town Peterborough recommendation to the City of Peterborough is to set a goal to become a net-positive renewable power generation community by 2035.

Chapter 3 covers the TTP concept proposal made to the City of Peterborough to kick-start local investment in local renewable power. This proposal represents only one financing model as an option because the funds from the sale of PDI to Hydro One were at hand. Pending the outcome of this recommendation, TTP will propose a green-energy bond model already suggested in the verbal commentary of the PowerPoint presentation made to the PDI Investment Options Working Group.

ECONOMIC LOCALIZATION INFRASTRUCTURE REGENERATIVE SYSTEM:

Kawartha Loon local currency:

January 23, 2021. We live in a country where most people rarely think about the fundamentals of the economic system in which we live, and worse than that, their eyes very often glaze over when you try to speak about economics. Having given many town halls, workshops, and one-on-one pitches on the Kawartha Loon local currency at our two local festivals each year, I know what it feels like, after explaining how a complementary currency actual works and that it is perfectly legal, when folks say... isn't that interesting and then walk away. It's frustrating at the very least and takes perseverance to keep talking about something over and over and expecting different results. I know that's the definition of insanity that most people attribute to Albert Einstein, my greatest hero when it comes to energy.

There are even some people who have the wild idea that TTP is somehow making money off the KL when the key benefit is actually to increase the local economic multiplier effect. In plain language, it's to keep more money in the community for a longer period of time to generate more transactions in the currency, thereby boosting economic localization and leading ultimately to greater local prosperity and more local sustainable jobs and livelihoods.

So, the KL is all about local residents buying from locally owned businesses and those businesses trading with each other in KLs in the Peterborough Community and thereby increasing the store of value of the community that actually backs the currency. This store of value in the local community builds community resilience and eventually encourages local residents who have investment funds in both Canadian dollars and KLs to invest in their own community in real estate and locally owned businesses as they currently do, but also in investment opportunities that localize more and more of our life essentials.

The community at large is the beneficiary of a growing store of value as it leads to an enhanced property tax base providing the municipal funds to deliver the services the community needs. This represents a very brief outline of how local economies can work to enhance the real value of the community and the happiness of those who live in it. It also suggests the logical next step for the system is to become regenerative and the community even more resilient. In the case of the City and County of Peterborough, they need to find ways to accept payment for services including some portion of property taxes in KLs. This could include the issuing of green bonds in KLs with the interest paid in KLs. The bonds could be used to build new solar power generation plants or biogas plants, a consumers' or farmers' co-op for local food or a new sports & entertainment centre in downtown Peterborough as a necessary part of our culture.

Transition Town Peterborough can't take on the job alone of scaling the KL to community size nor can we leave it as is, as a boutique currency waiting for someone to do the job for us after the next local climate change emergency, the pending energy crisis or currency crisis when it is needed even more.

Rather What if---

- Transition Town Peterborough transferred the issuer of the currency to PKED or to any other entity owned jointly by the City and County of Peterborough such as a Trust as was suggested in the original TTP document leading to the introduction of the Kawartha Loon. That City & County entity would receive the interest on the reserve held by the banking agent(s) that sold the currency into existence with zero transaction fees in order to secure the reserve for their institution. The exchange rate between the Canadian Dollar and the KL is determined by the Board of Governors of the Kawartha Loon Exchange (KLE) which would also be passed to the new entity.

- Peterborough & the Kawarthas Economic Development or other entities were assigned, budgeted and staffed by the City

& County of Peterborough to scale the KL to community size with the objective of growing the members of the KLE to 50% of all of the locally owned businesses and farming enterprises in three years. All of the KLE members as qualified are engaged in providing the local community life essentials, including public housing, food, water, energy, culture and wellness. PKED or any other entity would need lots of big data to make that happen. Much of this data exists with Peterborough Chamber of Commerce, which is already a member of the KLE, and with PKED.

- Peterborough & Kawarthas Economic Development or other entity implements the TTP plan to convert the KL local currency to an electronic 5% discount loyalty program exclusive to the Peterborough Community and accepted only by locally owned businesses and farming enterprises and by the City and County for some services such as city water, dumping fees, fees for services at municipally owned facilities and some portion of property tax to begin with. The property tax payment level must grow in proportion to the growth of the store of value of the community as a whole. The TTP plan calls to maintain the print version as a security against the failure of the internet or any other crisis. The print version of the KL comes in denominations of $1, $2.50, $5, $10 and $20.

TTP already has the software license to implement the electronic version of the Kawartha Loon (eKL) and one local banking agent prepared to support the launch. The new eKL software is likely to be applicable to multiple Canadian banks.

So, what if we were to put this plan outline together; who in the City and County do we deliver it to?

Who is thinking about community resilience and local store of value post COVID-19?

The answers to those questions are currently being discussed among the members of the Kawartha Loon Exchange Board of Governors and the TTP Board of Directors. Is there any other way to scale to community size and embed the currency into the regeneration of the community through the economics of localization and happiness?

Investing, Buying, and Trading Locally:

This system clearly interconnects with the KL local currency for buying locally, However, for businesses who receive a large number of KLs, there has to be some other business willing to trade with them using Loons and ultimately somewhere for some businesses to actually invest their profits held in Loons to create the long-term community store of value that is needed to help create the community resilience needed to allow the community to bounce forward after a crisis.

Needless to say, the same system could work with the Canadian dollar, but globalization has taken that away from us. We long to buy, buy, buy the latest gizmo online and have it delivered to our door with three days free shipping, never mind how much energy the whole transaction takes and never mind where the profits from the transaction end up. A simple basic understanding of how money flows would conclude that not much if any of the purchase price ends up in the pockets of local citizens.

Maybe with a little luck the package arrives by Canada Post and you know the driver by name, and the driver lives in the local community; but most often it's directly from an out-of-town warehouse with a driver who has never lived locally, who was guided by GPS to deliver your package within one hour of the advanced electronic delivery notification via your smartphone--- pretty cool, eh! Yes, until something messes up in the transaction and you want to send it back or you want to talk to someone on how to hook it up or put it together. "That shouldn't be a problem, sir," says the voice on the other end of the line who speaks English with an almost musical accent that you can't quite understand. He lives in India, of course; not that there is anything wrong with that! Right?

I bring you this one simple example of how communities continue the practice of their own citizens hollowing- out their own community and wondering why all the small locally owned businesses that at one time flourished here have closed their doors. The point is that options exist, including the KL to motivate local citizens to buy local to help build the store of value and community resilience that can regenerate itself and bounce forward as a community after the next disruption.

That reminds me of the ridiculous debate that our current City Council had over the proposal to reduce the run hours of the water fountain in Little Lake in the centre of the downtown core. The store of value of that fountain in its representation of Peterborough was too great to overlook in the interest of saving the electrical energy. Of course, there was no mention of what makes up a real store of value in 2020 and store of value was never mentioned. It was all plain old emotional opinions from everyone on Council to debate this one-off issue.

Before moving to the investment part of the "Investing, Buying and Trading Locally Regenerative System," I present a quote from the book *Local Dollars, Local Sense: A Community Resilience Guide* by Michael Shuman, Copyright 2012, of the Post Carbon Institute:

> *"Every job in a locally owned business generates two to four times as much economic-development benefits as a job in an equivalent non-local business. Local businesses spend more money locally, which helps to pump up what is known as the local economic multiplier. The more times a given dollar circulates in a community and the faster it circulates without leaking out, the more income, wealth, and jobs are created in that community. That's the cornerstone of all economic development. What we now know, beyond any doubt, is that local businesses do this better than non-locals."*

Clarifying the quotation a little, a local business is one owned by one or more people who live in the community, and certainly not the local big-box retailers who have stores in the local community.

Local Investing:

Apart from small business owners, and the light commercial buildings they occupy along with residential homes, and locally owned rental apartments, there are few opportunities in Peterborough for a small- to medium-sized investor to invest locally.

Among the existing opportunities, the residential home real estate market is the most vibrant regenerative system. Even it has become a very difficult market in which to safely invest. Home prices are on the rise from out of town older often retired people cashing out their homes in bigger cities and moving to Peterborough making it much more difficult for local young people, thinking about new family formation, to assemble down payments for housing in their own community.

This was the traditional way to live, raise a family, accumulate a little investment capital and become invested in the community in which they lived. Globalization has caused this idealistic scenario to mostly disappeared in Peterborough, changing everything from health care to recreation, entertainment, sense of place and commitment to belonging. Indeed, just like every other community in Canada, the residents of Peterborough live here physically but are addicted to the hype of technology and globalization. Beyond their home, they have no idea where their investments are and they mostly don't care to understand the relevance.

If they do have some idea it will likely be about not investing in oil because fossil fuels cause emissions that have created the climate crisis. I'm not certain if most homeowners in the City of Peterborough who heat with natural gas realize that natural gas is a fossil fuel and will soon have to be replaced. Residents in the County beyond the fringe of the City, continue to be mostly heating with propane but you can see more and more neat piles of wood for backup heating.

The fast-rising local residential home prices change the community demographics and the type of available jobs in the community, making the community as a whole less resilient, and more in need of rental housing for lower-income people.

And yet, to build a local resilient community with a significant store of value requires a large percentage of the working population living here to also be invested in their own community. There are now few credit unions that actually invest all their funds in the local economy in which they are located. They have been forced to merge with other credit unions in order to keep up with the big banks on the technology-driven services provided to customers. Further, in Peterborough, there are very few co-operatives as compared to other parts of Canada.

If a local resident did have $1,000 to $50,000 to invest in their own community how would they locate a sound and safe investment? Globalization and the big banks have taken that opportunity away. Their local bank branch no longer has a branch manager to talk to. The resident still has their money there in GICs or Tax-Free Savings Accounts or RRSPs, but who knows where their money goes. None of those options make the resident feel good about investing in their own community.

So, what about green-energy bonds for local citizens to invest in their own community's energy security? This opportunity was proposed in Chapter 3: Renewable Power Generation Investment Trust Fund and could apply not only to the local renewable energy sector but to local food and local culture, among the life essentials with the use of co-operatives, and even to locally owned business in any sector.

If enough companies were taking up the model suggested in Chapter 3 we would need a local bond exchange for local investors to invest in local business, developing another means to keep the money generated here in the local community. Clearly, some of the bonds could be denominated in KLs with the interest paid on the bonds denominated in KLs.

The City & County of Peterborough could issue green bonds denominated in KLs to become a dynamic part of the system to keep much more money circulating locally.

We have the power to build our own resilient community with the money we have. All we have to do is figure out ways to keep it here. This is the objective of the KL local currency and of the whole idea of building our own economic localization infrastructure which in the end leads to more jobs and livelihoods and the economics of happiness.

Local Food, Water and Wellness:

Local food is by far the best understood, supporting regenerative system that needs to grow most quickly to become a significant part of the economic localization regenerative system in the City and County of Peterborough. We must be in a position to feed ourselves by 2035 from a very low base in early 2021 as the risk of not doing so becomes more and more apparent with the area becoming one of the most food-insecure communities in Canada as amplified by COVID-19.

It's all about how to bring locally grown food to the front and centre of the City and County Councils to provide the funding to build the regenerative local food systems.

After 13 years of support for local food, we transitioners know that the City and County have no official jurisdiction over local food. There is no responsibility under the Municipal Act for the City or County with respect to any food source. There is no line-item budgetary amount for local food anywhere in the City or County annual budgets, whereas there is a line-item budget in both the City and County in support of PKED, the jointly financed Economic Development Organization.

Peterborough & the Kawarthas Economic Development has a history of playing at the fringes of local food, mostly helping local farmers create directories, but PKED has never had a serious plan to increase the production of local food that was fully supported by City and County funding, nor a serious plan to reduce already existing carbon emissions in the air that could take place if the permaculture method of growing food was also employed.

If you were to approach PKED in the past with respect to local food and indeed economic localization infrastructure and the KL local currency, their interest would have been polite, but the only frank feedback would be that they had never had a budget to cover the idea being presented, then apart from participating in their third 5-year plan update, we would never hear from them again on the topic.

Certainly, we still haven't heard from anyone at PKED during the pandemic and yet this entity remains the last best hope to develop the local food system which is of critical importance for the Peterborough Community to become a much more resilient community.

Meanwhile, because the City and County have signed onto the Sustainable Peterborough Plan (SPP) that says that we need to feed ourselves by the mid-2030s, the City provides very modest funding for some things, such as the Purple Onion Harvest Festival and Local Food Month, Community Gardens and Pollinator Gardens and a few of the local farmers' markets by providing them with outdoor spaces with reasonable rental rates. The City and County both give their praises to the local Food Banks even though they rarely pass out nutritious local food. Quite the contrary, the entire community supports passing out the unhealthiest foods available to the less fortunate. How do we overlook that societal crime against our own residents?

The local Health Unit knows that you can't separate personal or community wellness from the food we consume, and they have been actively engaged in nutritious local food for at least as many years as TTP. But the Health Unit continues with two disadvantages: they have no jurisdiction over food and no money as a function of the Province of Ontario, which for the most part is interested only in the export value of all foods grown in Ontario and the jobs that supports. There is no interest in the soil and how food is grown on the soil, only a designation rating of the suitability of the land for agriculture or green space and what types of buildings you are allowed to build on the land for what use. A farmer is free to build the soil or devastate the soil as most have done for generations. There are no jurisdictions or laws over how our farmers manage their own soil, and indeed there are few best practices shared to rebuild the soil in the area in view of the observable rapidly changing climate.

Indeed, how do we design the systems to develop much greater food security, create many more local jobs and livelihoods at a living wage without the financial support from the City and County? The answer is we can't likely make it happen without a huge influx of operational and capital funding from both the City and County, which will require significant changes in the way both those bodies operate. It should go without saying at this point that the task would be much easier if the City and County were to adopt permaculture as their operating systems as proposed in this book.

Before further developing the design of a local food regenerative system for our Peterborough Community, I want to take you back to Chapter 4: Strategic Roadmap, specifically Section J Environment.

Herein lies a quotation by Kristin Ohlson from her beautiful book titled *The Soil Will Save Us* that speaks to food security and the major way to reduce future carbon emissions and the ones that are already in the air: *"To be sure, we must continue to cut back on fossil-fuel use and lead less squandering lives. But we also have to extract excess carbon from the atmosphere by working with photosynthesis instead of against it."*

As Kristin Ohlson discusses in this same book, before the First Industrial Revolution:

> *"People weren't driving cars and tearing the tops off of mountains to mine coal for electric power, but they burned forests to create pastureland and cropland, and then ripped open the soil with increasingly damaging plows to plant their crops. They didn't pave paradise, but there was so much of it that they could afford to ruin one plot of ground and just move on to the next green space."*

What we learn from Kristin Ohlson's book is that down through the ages our destructive agriculture practices utilized in our continuing search for more food have released much of the carbon that existed in the soil into the air. Carbon-rich soil is black like carbon. Some of that carbon released from the soil has been absorbed into our oceans and is destructively increasing ocean acidification, thus contributing to the reduction of the bounty from them.

Further, we learn that the most effective way to reduce the carbon released from growing food is, in Transition-Town speak, to utilize permaculture practices to grow our food. Even further, Kristin Ohlson is saying to us that those same practices are also the best way to extract the carbon emissions that we humans have already put into the atmosphere. That is, use photosynthesis to grow food in such a way that holds carbon in the soil and actually reduces the amount of carbon that already exists in the air from the worst practices of all mankind.

When you think of this scenario presented by Kristin Ohlson, have a look at all the research references in her book. If you can put yourself in the shoes of Ted Turner, as previously represented in this chapter, as he looks out over his grassy plains with buffalo running free-range, you can admire and be gratified by the proof positive of this direction.

Now in Canada, we have the A & W fast food chain advertising free-range beef grown in Canada with no additives given to the cattle or anything added to the land. The announcer in the Ad interviews the farmers who have supposedly raised the cattle and poses the question: You really are grass farmers then. Is that right? They answer in the affirmative. I realize that the Ad could be all show but the fast-food chain is at least thinking about how it can differentiate its product with better more nutritious food. It's a trend that I believe is catching on. If the fast-food chain finds out that those grassy fields are also the best, fastest and least expensive way to sequester, through photosynthesis the CO_2 that already exists in the air we might have something. You do have to keep the herd size in balance though. The cattle expel methane which is much more lethal as a GHG than CO_2.

My point here is that with free-range food moving more to the mainstream, we can't be too far away from how we need to live and grow our food, and for that matter work on ways to reduce the amount of CO_2 already in the atmosphere.

One more little story. In the winter of 2019 we kicked off our first of five public sessions on building a more resilient Peterborough by 2030. We had formed a small group of four people to lead the sessions and provide some stimulation to the group. These four people included a United Church minister whose major interest was social equity. He had a reasonable understanding of the Transition Town model and an interest in growing food and working together. The second person was a professional facilitator who volunteered his services. He knew something about Transition Town through other community gatherings that he had facilitated but was far from a transitioner in our estimation and as we found out later was not even aware of permaculture. The third person was our director of permaculture operations, and the fourth was yours truly. We opened each evening with a 15-minute presentation on the topic of the evening. The first session was on permaculture. Our permaculturalist as titled above explained the basics of the permaculture operating system. She took many questions and took longer than 15 minutes before we moved into the breakouts.

I suppose that it was difficult for some including our facilitator that we would consider permaculture the most critical understanding to advance on the energy crisis, economic crisis, and the resulting climate crisis. At the end of the session, the new TTP facilitator asked what turned out to be a standard question for all sessions. How important is tonight's topic to you and our community?

The facilitator was baffled by our permaculturalist's response that permaculture as our operating system was the absolute most important and critical consideration for our future progress as a community.

There was no vote, but the notion of its critical importance carried that evening as it does now to add some considerable credibility to the idea of developing a permaculture local food system for the City and County of Peterborough.

As with Ted Turner's grasslands permaculture design, even when left almost 100% to nature with photosynthesis, a system takes some time to mature, but we can learn rather quickly and introduce rather quickly and get started rather quickly if we have the will to make a difference in the security of our own lives.

Our proposal to the City and County of Peterborough is to assign the development of local food to PKED with the understanding that they will use permaculture as the driving modus operandi.

To start up the new assignment, PKED should be prepared to re-assign at least two individuals from within including a local food leader and a communications manager and begin to recruit at least three permaculture certified specialists: one for the overall design, one for water and soil management and the third for pollination. This would create a team of five people fully budgeted in response to the City's own declaration of a climate emergency and in recognition of one of the City's best-known naturalists, Drew Monkman, who has recently reported on how quickly the climate has already changed in the Peterborough Area.

This group's first assignment would be to outreach to all the groups in the community engaged in local food including TTP and form a task force to put together all the requirements to achieve 50% local food by 2030; a goal already set by TTP.

Transition Town has a research project underway at the TCRC by that name and we welcome PKED to join with us to help guide the fourth-year student that has taken the project on.

Project #4944 is titled "50% Local Food 2030 Economic Impact Analysis and Supply Chain Requirements (both economic and physical infrastructure)."

All of the ideas including capital projects, as shown in Chapter 4: Strategic Roadmap, such as the Regional Food Hub and the purchase of several farms for start-up food co-ops will be reviewed in this project.

Water: Reliable, safe drinking water is thought to be a human right by most Canadians. However here we are in Peterborough County, as recently announced with the Curve Lake First Nations Chief who is also a lawyer, that she is now a leading representative plaintiff in a class-action lawsuit filed in federal court over the lack of safe drinking for First Nations across Canada. The Curve Lake Chief argues that her local community has been without consistently safe drinking water for over 30 years.

This is disgraceful for a country like Canada to have taken so much from Indigenous peoples and still consistently fail them, especially at a time when we need their knowledge base to live in much greater harmony with nature over generations to come; indeed, the next seven generations.

Wellness: The whole idea of wellness as part of a permaculture system may be new to most people who read this book. But we transitioners in Peterborough adopted the idea very early on and cultivated the Dandelion Day Festival as our celebration of wellness making the dandelion our symbol.

We had a lot of fun with the symbol in costume, on T-Shirts and hats and discussion with folks who came to the festival---many with the implanted idea that the dandelion was a weed that you needed to kill with Round Up and get out of your lawn. Some conversations were full of laughter and information; others made us think that some people were coming to the festival to find a legal spray to eradicate them from their property. The positives were greater than the negatives and we featured the bright yellow flower on our *Greenzine* magazine cover more than once.

The dandelion flower blooms everywhere in Southern Ontario in the early spring. The leaves are edible and nutritional and many of the older folks in the area remember making dandelion wine from the whole plant when there was no source of grapes. Although in this area, wild grapes grow everywhere clinging to bushes and trees extending 20 feet high and sometimes more than 100 feet from a plant's root.

There are many front and back yards that in early spring break into a sea of yellow flowers. The dandelion lives on; the green leaves now show up for sale at conventional grocery stores, and not that there is a causal relationship here, but we probably have 15 naturopathic doctors in the community whereas we only had three at the start-up of TTP in 2007. At one point, we transitioners started the all-volunteer Transition Wellness Institute to complement the all-volunteer Transition Skills Forum, but the community is still not big enough to keep it going. What we have observed but not yet researched to verify is that the wellness sector is likely the second-largest new job creator in our community after local food.

Together, local food, water and wellness all driven by permaculture design practices offer the largest opportunity for new sustainable jobs and livelihoods in our community.

Downtown Culture Hub:

There are only two states for consideration of downtown areas across Canada: before COVID-19 and after COVID-19.

Before the pandemic, Downtown Peterborough was starting to show some signs of revival. Lots of work was yet to be done but the arts and culture community was blossoming again. The independent restaurants were a major attraction, several new apartment blocks bringing more people to the downtown area had recently been completed and new ones were on the drawing board. The car remained dominant, and business owners called out for more downtown parking, but bicycle lanes seemed to service most of the downtown area. The new outdoor home for the downtown Wednesday Farmers' Market was finally under construction. Public transportation remained inadequate, but the great debate had begun as to whether or not the new sports and entertainment centre would be built in the downtown core or farther away in Morrow Park where, in a different era, the local agriculture society ran a hugely successful county fair with a carnival component. That fair, as the event of the year for many local generations, had long passed its best use before date.

Now on January 25, 2021, as we pass into the second year of the virus with new strains being discovered, Peterborough, Ontario, received its first shipment of vaccine--- It is from Moderna.

The community remains under an Ontario provincial government stay-at-home order with only essential services open. And you can't actually shop in most of the essential service stores. We are down to call ahead and curbside pick-up for almost everything needed. The downtown area certainly loses the competitive battle to the out-of-town strips that exist in Peterborough when it comes to this service brought to us by the virus.

The downtown area including the new sports and entertainment centre project needed lots of help before COVID-19 and will need it even more when the pandemic is over. However, what it looks like to me is that we will be into municipal elections in 2022 and the political posturing will soon start delaying the revitalization of the downtown area for four years in total.

Peterborough is a relatively small town. Transition Town Peterborough is vested in support of the downtown locally owned businesses, with the KL local currency, the Downtown Culinary Hub, the circulation of the *Greenzine* magazine and our two annual festivals---one for local food and the other for local wellness.

The downtown hub can rise and bounce forward after the pandemic; it's likely the first resiliency challenge posed from within the City's own climate emergency. We hope that you see it as such as alluded to in this book and with specific recommendations in Chapter 4. We in Transition Town are anxiously awaiting the making of the case that the downtown hub needs the KL local currency and a robust dedication to local food to revitalize itself and become a driver of much greater economic localization.

ENVIRONMENTAL REGENERATIVE SYSTEMS:

The City and County of Peterborough located as the entry into the Kawarthas are not only capable of becoming a net positive renewable energy community by 2035 as communicated in this book, but it is also well-positioned to become a net-positive carbon sink by 2035.

What this means is that the soil and plants covering the area, through photosynthesis, will absorb more carbon than the area emits into the air each year from cars, trucks and farm equipment, home and commercial heating and cooling, etc. This should be our goal. There is a huge requirement for big data to support our progress towards this goal. This goal can only be put together by permaculturists working with all the farmers, construction companies building new subdivisions leaving piles of topsoil exposed to the sun's radiation and serious efforts to de-pave the City as is already going on in the downtown area as supported by the DBIA; and by partnering with neighbourhoods with small grants to replace paved driveways with sponge driveways allowing water to pass into the soil in place rather than go into the storm water system.

Within the Peterborough Community area, there appears to be more room for parks and more designated wilderness areas with minimal pathways.

For any environmental initiative to be visibly regenerative, it has to cover the ground with vegetation. This applies to farming too. Regenerative farming is an intermediate step to permaculture food forests and likely where we will need to advance to between now and 2035, the time set to feed ourselves in the Peterborough Community. There are a lot of farms in the area already building the soil-maintaining cover crops and managing their source of water. The TTP recommendation to move the leadership of the 50% Local Food 2030 project to PKED and hiring the permaculturalists to get the job done is consistent with the area striving to be a net carbon sink.

EQUITY REGENERATIVE SYSTEMS:

The only way to accomplish significant gains in social and economic equity in the Peterborough Community and any other community is to build equity into all the other systems that need to be implemented to build a more resilient community. The very simple way to describe this is that if everyone is not part of the solution, the problem will not likely go away. The COVID-19 pandemic is a prime example: to be blunt, it doesn't care how much money you have.

One of the finest examples of this philosophy is Habitat For Humanity's two ReStores in the community supported by donations from the general public and staffed mostly by volunteers. The funds from the stores go towards building modest lower-income family homes, supported by their own sweat equity. In my mind, this is almost a perfect model of working together with social and economic equity.

The one area of concern that I have with respect to all local charities, including Habitat for Humanity, the Peterborough Foundation, and others is that they don't really know where their financial reserves are invested and what they are supporting for so little return. In my estimation, they need to spend more time thinking about how to integrate in balance with the four E's on the key regenerative systems that blend to create a more resilient community.

A key regenerative system that speaks to this concern is investing, buying, trading locally.

If we think about investing locally, local charities, including churches carry bank balances beyond their working capital requirements. These reserves often just sit in bank accounts with very little return and with no idea how their respective banks or other institutions are using these funds. They could be invested in oil, who knows, but they are most certainly not invested locally. Indeed, the City has huge amounts of reserves that are invested outside the community, likely restricted by the Municipality Act in some way, but I can't imagine that with a little creativity that couldn't be changed. There are countless ideas available on how to reverse the flow of money from communities like Peterborough.

We have all been duped by the global financial system to the point that the system has less and less to do with the real economy where most of us actually live---locally. So we need to pull our reserves away from Wall Street and Bay Street and put them to work locally to create a more resilient community that is also more equitable.

Reinforcing the point, there are reserve funds created in and by the community that have nowhere to go but outside the community for very low return. To achieve any kind of lasting community resilience requires that we all invest in our own community that we are hoping to build and enjoy. We have to start talking about this and not allow the global financial system trajectory it is on to crash and take all the local reserves with it.

The challenge put forward in this book is to build the local investment infrastructure in Peterborough starting with bonds for local renewable power generation startups; and the use of our own KL local currency to increase the economic multiplier effect. As a bit of an advertising commercial for the KL local currency--- if you are donating money to any charity or part, you are part of a charity giving small amounts of cash to the public. So give it in Kawartha Loons and help your community become a little more resilient!

I had a little fun with this during the last federal election. I had four political parties requesting donations from me. Two of the four consistently had booths at our annual Purple Onion Harvest Festival and supported the KL. It has always been our policy that if you had a political agenda you needed to purchase booth space to advocate the same. It seems that all political parties are for local food and local wellness until they have to advocate to put more money into these systems.

To be fair, I said to all four political parties that I would give each of them 100 KLs but as a legal complementary currency to the Canadian dollar, I wanted the receipt in Canadian dollars so that I could deduct it from my federal income taxes. Only one of them was able to figure out how to handle the KL and got me my receipt for $100 Canadian without messing up their donation books. I saved 300 KLs on that election.

All of the regenerative systems covered in this book require equitable integration. Two more significant ones for some commentary are the availability of low-cost public transportation, which in TTP is part of the local renewable power regenerative system, and local food, water, and wellness regenerative system.

Dealing with public transportation first, the entire system needs to be electrified by 2035 and run with locally generated renewable power. This is also the date when new fossil fuel cars in Canada will likely be banned for sale, assuming we follow the California environmental regulations as we are now. This is also the date advocated by TTP to become a net positive renewable power generation community. Further, the City public transportation system needs to be accepting the KL local currency in both electronic and print form and transportation passes should be available in the KL.

Transition Town Peterborough has made several representations for electrified public transportation, as have other groups with no official feedback. The City has just accepted federal funds to support the purchase of more fossil fuel buses. Without knowing the useful life of these buses, it is difficult to determine if the purchase is justified. The first City move on electrification of public transportation will likely be indicated by how the funds from the sale of PDI are invested. If a high percentage of these funds are invested into the local renewable power generation system as recommended in Chapter 3, then we will present our proposal, yet again, for an equitable electrified public transportation system that will encourage homeowners and renters alike to leave their electric cars at home and venture to the downtown hub for cultural and culinary satisfaction, hopefully for years to come.

The local food, water and wellness regenerative system is the key to reducing food insecurity in the community. The permaculture designed local food system doesn't eliminate all mechanization but what it does is pull all the steps from the industrial food supply chain into a local food supply chain and works on preserving water, building the soil, and maximizing the possible yield.

This alone allows a good percentage of the farmers' yield, before processing, to be sold directly to the consumer, increasing the resilience of the system often described as from farm to fork. With rising industrial food prices caused by our changing climate, irrigation water availability and currency fluctuations with every foreign country supplying food to our local citizens, there will be a point when local food becomes less expensive than imported industrial food. Weather patterns are changing so quickly, making the growing of traditional crops more difficult, again supporting permaculture principles that build the soil leading to the highest yield.

Feeding ourselves by 2035 will take millions of dollars of capital and operational funding, most certainly for a local food hub and multiple co-operative farms in the area training new young farmers while producing a monetary return on the food they grow. Some of these recommendations have been presented earlier in the book. The reality is that if we are unable to figure out how to feed ourselves as suggested in the Sustainable Peterborough Plan approved by the City and County of Peterborough and First Nations and created at taxpayer expense, it will likely be nearly impossible to save the community from a downward spiral full of inequity and outright poverty.

PETERBOROUGH COMMUNITY GOALS:

The following goals will be achieved with the advancement of the permaculture regenerative systems:

- Most Resilient Community in Canada by 2030

- Net-Positive Renewable Energy Community by 2035

- Net-Positive Carbon Sink Community by 2035

- Electrify all public transportation using local renewable energy by 2035

- 50% Local Food by 2030

- Feed ourselves with local food by 2035 as approved in the Sustainable Peterborough Plan, by the City and County of Peterborough and First Nations.

CHAPTER 8 ██████████████

MY LAST WORDS

Jan 30, 2021: My last words are for hope for our collective futures in Peterborough, Ontario, Canada, and around the world.

Overshadowing this is the arrival of the South African COVID-19 variant in the US and Canada which is bringing into question the effectiveness of existing vaccines and whether or not new versions will be able to keep up with the new virus variants fast enough to achieve some level of global herd immunity this year. The longer the virus controls our lives, the more difficult it becomes to bounce forward with adaptive changes that address the climate crisis.

On the climate crisis front, NASA reports that 2020 was the hottest year on record but an effective tie with 2016, with satellite images of raging fires in Australia, California and Siberia marking the year, like annual growth rings in a tree.

Some good news on the climate crisis science is that if we can reduce GHG emissions to net-zero the planetary warming trend may well level off *"within a decade or two"* as reported by Dr. Joeri Rogeli, a climate scientist and leading author of the next major climate assessment from the IPCC.

I hope Dr. Rogeli's assertions turn out to pass all the scientific scrutiny of the IPCC before an official announcement is made. Although a positive development for humans, it may very well delay global action to achieve net-zero GHG emissions by 2050.

China has already pushed their zero-carbon achievement plan from 2050 to 2060, and I expect that their scientific analysis indicates little hope to reach zero global emissions by 2060 without a significant global population decline coupled with a significant global per capita energy usage reduction, requiring significant lifestyle changes for all of humanity.

My last words summarize my story ...

Photosynthesis, permaculture, life essentials, energy descent, local renewable energy, changing lifestyles, local resilience, economic localization infrastructure, local currencies, investing, buying and trading locally, environmental regeneration, social, racial and economic equity, lots of local food, mixed with hope, celebration, determination, municipal leadership, locally owned businesses and citizen engagement focused on the economics of happiness.

Together we can!

NOTES AND REFERENCES

INTRODUCTION

Biden-Harris ticket: Joe Biden and Kamala Harris campaign for President and Vice President of the United States of America in 2020.

Net-zero carbon emissions: The reference refers to the aggregate of all greenhouse gas emissions being zero. The net refers to a particular area or country where the absorption of emissions from the air through photosynthesis offsets the new emissions, delivering a net of zero carbon emissions.

Vote of no confidence in Canadian parliamentary system: A vote of the majority of the members of the House of Commons against the government, usually on a throne speech or a budgetary bill forcing a new election.

Fiat Currency: Currency such as the Canadian and US dollars that have no intrinsic value and are actually only backed by the store of value of the country issuing the currency.

KL local currency issued by TTP: The Kawartha Loon local currency is a complementary currency to the Canadian dollar that can be converted to the Canadian dollar at any time at the exchange rate established by Kawartha Loon Exchange Board of Governors as part of Transition Town Peterborough Inc. At scale to the Peterborough Community at large, the backing of the KL becomes the store of value of the community in which it circulates.

Transitioners: This is the adopted name of people who follow the Transition Towns movement, at least in Peterborough, Ontario, Canada.

CHAPTER 1

Gaia: The Gaia hypothesis, originated by James Lovelock, suggests that the earth behaves like a complex self-correcting living system regulating its own temperature as does the human body.

Cyber warfare: Refers to digital attacks causing disruption to computer systems equivalent to that caused by wars in the physical world.

Andrea Bocceli: Italian opera tenor who became totally blind at age 12.

Hydro One: Incorporated in Ontario, majority-owned by the Province of Ontario and the largest electric distribution company in the province.

CHAPTER 2

PR: Public Relations

Rare earths: Refers to a group of rare earth elements REEs that are necessary for the manufacture of all sorts of high-tech devices from cell phones to computers to wind power generators to electric cars.

Two countries in the world namely China and Canada have the bulk of these rare earths, many of which are needed to implement the new green economy.

5G: Represents the fifth generation of technology for broadband cellular networks offering much higher capacity and speed. It's the first generation to be designed with more than phones in mind so it is intended to bring a whole new set of applications and innovation around the Internet of Things.

IoT: Internet of Things ..... The physical things connected by the internet

Jeremy Rifkin books and the Internet of Things: Rifkin is the author of over 25 books at least three of which are relevant to the Transition Towns model as interpreted in this book: *The Third Industrial Revolution*, *The Green New Deal*, and *The Zero Marginal Cost Society*. The IoT refers to the physical things that are embedded with sensors and software or otherwise connected over the internet.

Nuclear fusion vs nuclear fission: Nuclear fusion is the process that takes place in the sun and all the stars to produce energy. From a layperson's point of view, we can think of this as a nuclear reaction between light elements to form heavier elements and in the process release enormous amounts of energy. This has never been commercialized although NASA reported in 2020 the demonstration of fusion on a tiny scale.

Nuclear fission is the process utilized with all commercialized nuclear reactors on the planet. The technology is based on splitting the nucleus of an atom into two or more smaller, lighter nuclei and capturing the huge amount of energy released in the process.

Feasibility question: Transition Town Peterborough generally uses a four-phase program planning process including concept/feasibility/design and implementation. This process seems to be well understood by local businesses and the City of Peterborough. A detailed financial and engineering analysis and some expert feedback assessment are included in this phase and if a project can't satisfy the questions raised at this phase it will likely be scrapped.

Transition Neighbourhoods Project (TNP): This is the proprietary Transition Towns' energy descent project modified by Transition Town Peterborough to suit the Peterborough Community.

Greater Peterborough Area: Refers to the Peterborough community or the Peterborough Census Metropolitan Area (CMA), which includes all of the City of Peterborough and parts of the surrounding area in the County of Peterborough.

Grid: Refers to the centralized system of wires, poles, transformers and other equipment employed to deliver most of Ontario's electricity as owned by Hydro One.

Elite 1%: As a measure of inequality the top 1% of Americans held 30.4% of household wealth in the US, while a Credit Suisse report pegs the global 1% household wealth at 50.4% of the global total in 2020.

House in the casino economy: The house refers to the elite 1% who hold the power to control the global capitalistic system through central banks and other financial institutions.

Fracking producers: Companies engaged in fracking for oil and natural gas.

Quantitative easing: Described as QE. The US Federal Reserve system of increasing the liquidity in the private banking system.

Catch-22: A circumstance with no escape.

Food-waste bubble: The food along the food supply chain that is never consumed by people.

Oil cartel: A group of nations bound together to control the supply or prices of oil.

Supply bubble: Created when supply excessively exceeds demand.

Debt bubble: Occurs when total debt exceeds the ability to pay it down.

First Industrial Revolution: Believed to have started with the invention of the steam engine first driven by wood, then coal.

Bursting carbon bubble: The point when it is widely understood that 80% of the coal, natural gas and oil reserves must stay in the ground.

Paris COP 21: The 21st Conference of the Parties to the 1992 United Nations Framework Convention on Climate Change. It was held in Paris, France, and led to the Paris Climate Accord.

Pull ourselves up by our own economic bootstraps: Expression referring in this case to the community having to rely on its own economics for its own economic prosperity.

Black Friday: The Day after the US Thanksgiving which has spread into Canada as a major shopping day. It originated as the day in the year when retailers began to see positive earnings "in the black."

Green washed in reference to sustainability: Big businesses and governments alike have tried to position themselves as supporting the green environmental sustainability movement with all kinds of schemes of sustainable development and the like that do not, in reality, reduce carbon emissions.

Stern Review (2006): A 700-page review on the economics of climate change led by Economist Nicholas Stern and released by the UK government in 2006.

Oil Peaker: Nickname for someone who follows the study of peak oil.

Hubbert curve: References King Hubbert's 1956 presentation of the curve for oil as the method for predicting the likely production rate over time from any well.

Montreal Protocol: The international treaty adopted in Montreal in 1987 used to regulate the production and use of chemicals that contribute to the depletion of the earth's ozone layer.

The cliff is approaching at lightning speed: Expression used by the writer for which no source has been found to date. It means that things are happening so fast that they are literally out of control and we are approaching the point that we can't do anything about it. We are about to fall off the cliff.

PEAC: Committee of Council named the Peterborough Environmental Advisory Committee.

TCRC: Trent Community Research Centre. Third-year, fourth-year and master's students take on projects that support the community for course credit. Supervision is shared by a designated professor and the originator of the project, in this case TTP.

Green Up: The City of Peterborough's long-standing environmental organization. It is a charity also funded by government grants and by Peterborough Holdings, which is owned by the City of Peterborough.

FRG: For Our Grandchildren is a local environmental group.

CHAPTER 3

PDI: City-owned power distribution company recently sold to Hydro One.

Not-for-profit social enterprise: Transition Town Peterborough is a not-for-profit all-volunteer organization focused on building community resilience with the earnings from its initiatives, the primary source of which has been from *Greenzine* magazine.

Food co-ops with energy co-op components: An example of this would be a local food hub co-op with a different energy co-op on-site providing electricity from solar or biogas.

Energy descent: A net decline in the amount of energy consumed.

Ptbo Holdings: The name of the City of Peterborough-owned company that previously owned PDI and currently owns the Water Utility, the Peterborough Zoo, Ecology Park and multiple renewable power generation facilities in the community.

Legacy fund option: Legacy funds are generally set up to support the communities from which the original funds were derived. The question in this context is where the funds would be invested to generate the return to the Peterborough Community.

For-fee project operator: In the case of Ptbo Holdings, already operate multiple renewable energy sites and could also act as the operator for a fee for other groups, co-ops, and companies that own renewable power generation sites.

Local food hub: This would include an indoor/outdoor permanent farmers' market, cleaning, storage, local food restaurant, community meeting room and on-site source of energy.

PDI Investment Options Working Group: Committee of City of Peterborough Council charged to recommend the disposition of funds from the sale of PDI to Hydro One.

The Third Industrial Revolution: A new industrial revolution is underway as the book by that name written by Jeremy Rifkin 2011 describes.

Rob Hopkins: The founder of Transition Town Totnes in England, the first Transition Town in the world, also co-founder of the Transition Network that supports the international Transition Towns movement, and the author of many books including, *From What is to What if*, published in 2019.

CHAPTER 4

Sponge streets: Created when paved boulevards are removed and replaced with grass or plants and paved residential driveways are replaced with interlocking stones or other cover that allows water absorption in place.

Worker co-ops: Workers are owners and managers of the business.

Downtown core: The downtown area is often served by a business association.

Replacement Memorial Centre: The existing Memorial Centre houses the two most attended sports teams in the community, namely the Peterborough Petes Junior A Hockey Team and the Peterborough Lakers minor lacrosse team. Both require expanded facilities in a new Sports and Entertainment Centre.

Community well-being: CWB is a formalized method of assessing socio-economic well-being in Canadian Cities.

New Economy Coalition: An American non-profit organization working for a future where people, communities and ecosystems thrive and where capital is a tool of the people, not the other way around.

Post Carbon Institute: A think tank located in Oregon, USA, the go-to site for information and analysis on climate change, energy scarcity, long-term community resilience and thinking resilience. Rob Hopkins, founder of the Transition Towns movement is also a Fellow of the Post Carbon Institute.

Biogas: Anaerobic digester that produces a mixture of gases produced by the breakdown of organic matter in the absence of oxygen.

Geothermal energy: Thermal energy generated and stored in the Earth.

Amazon: A company that started out selling books online and shipping them directly to consumers in North America and now is the largest company in the world selling a wide range of consumer products delivered directly to consumers.

Off-grid power generation systems: Off-grid power generation would be servicing a local requirement.

Cavan Monaghan: The name of a township adjacent to the City of Peterborough.

Externalities: To our economic system, references the non-inclusion of polluting our air and water and other life essentials.

DNA: When something is in our DNA, it is thought to be a part of our very being.

CHAPTER 5

Disruptors: Such as COVID-19, rising GHG emissions, or racial inequity.

Disruptor triage: Triage is a medical term used in emergencies to help decide who to work on first in the best interest of saving lives. It is a useful tool for understanding the best actions to be taken during the climate, COVID-19, and social equity emergencies.

Everywhen and everywhere: Everything happens at the same time everywhere as is the nature of the climate crisis.

NFP Sector: Not for profit.

Marginal cost economy: Automation and robotics have brought us to this point, where once we have figured out how to make the first widget with automation and robotics, the cost of making many more of the same widgets is a fraction of the cost or at a marginal cost of the first.

Non-monetized food: Food grown for home consumption and not sold.

CHAPTER 6

FIRE sector: Finance, insurance and real estate sectors.

Duped: Slang for misled.

Global elite: Often referred to as the upper 1% in terms of net worth.

VOCs: Volatile organic compounds.

MAGA: "Make America Great Again." Former US President Trump's election slogan.

DOW: Dow Jones Industrial Average Index.

S&P: Standard & Poors 500 Index.

Gone Amok: Slang for things going wrong.

CANDU heavy water reactors: Deuterium reactors

Earth Hour: Organized by the Worldwide Fund of Nature to turn off the lights for one hour once per year, usually in March

Big data: Big data and analysis is now a big global industry.

Second Industrial Revolution: Thought to have started with the invention of the internal combustion engine fired by gasoline from the oil economy.

CHAPTER 7

CNN: Cable News Network

Store of value: Used to describe what backs- up a fiat currency.

Drew Monkman: Local Naturalist in Peterborough, Ontario, and co-author of The Big Book of Nature Activities.

GPS: Global Positioning System.

GICs: Guaranteed Income Certificates.

RRSPs: Canadian Registered Retirement Savings Plans similar to 401K Plans in the USA.

Local bond exchange: Similar to a stock exchange but in this case trading only local bonds.

Round Up: This is a Monsanto brand name for herbicides and includes genetically modified seeds.

Best before date: In food it is the date when the taste begins to become stale. The reference here refers to the entire event becoming less than current or up to date.

DBIA: Downtown Business Improvement Association.